EUGENE O'NEILL

Born in New York City in 1888, son of a well-known actor, Eugene O'Neill spent a year at Princeton University (1906) before signing on as a seaman and travelling widely. Following a period in a sanatorium recovering from TB, he wrote his first play, *A Wife for a Life*. In 1916 he joined the Provincetown Players, who produced the first of his plays to be staged, *Bound East for Cardiff*, as well as other early work. His Broadway debut came in 1920 with *Beyond the Horizon*, which also won him a Pulitzer Prize.

The next fourteen years saw the premieres of some twenty new plays, including *The Emperor Jones* (1920), *Anna Christie* (1921), which won a second Pulitzer Prize, *The Hairy Ape* (1922), *All God's Chillun Got Wings* (1924), *Desire Under the Elms* (1924), *The Great God Brown* (1926), *Strange Interlude* (1928), which won another Pulitzer, *Mourning Becomes Electra* (1931), a trilogy reworking the *Oresteia*, *Ah! Wilderness* (1933) and *Days Without End* (1933), after which thirteen years elapsed with no new play reaching the stage, though he continued writing. Two more plays were produced during his lifetime: *The Iceman Cometh* in 1946, though written in 1939, and *A Moon for the Misbegotten* in 1947, though it only reached Broadway ten years later, after his death in 1953.

Plays staged posthumously include *Long Day's Journey Into Night* (1956), which won a fourth Pulitzer, *A Touch of the Poet* (1958) and *More Stately Mansions* (1962). He was three times married, his third wife, Carlotta Monterey, surviving him. In 1936 he became the first American dramatist to win the Nobel prize for Literature.

EUGENE O'NEILL
LONG DAY'S JOURNEY INTO NIGHT

Introduction by
Christine Dymkowski

NICK HERN BOOKS

Long Day's Journey Into Night first published in this edition in
1991, jointly by the Royal National Theatre, London,
and Nick Hern Books Limited, 14 Larden Road, London W3 7ST

This edition reprinted 1993, 1998, 1999, 2000, 2003, 2004, 2006

First published in Great Britain by Jonathan Cape in 1956

Cover photograph of Eugene O'Neill by courtesy of
the Raymond Mander & Joe Mitchenson Theatre Collection

Set in Baskerville by Tek Art Ltd, Addiscombe, Croydon, Surrey
Printed and bound in Great Britain by Cox & Wyman Ltd,
Reading, Berkshire

British Library Cataloguing in Publication Data

O'Neill, Eugene, *1888-1953*
Long day's journey into night.
    1. English drama. United States
    I. Title
    812.52

    ISBN-13 978 1 85459 102 9
    ISBN-10 1 85459 102 9

Contents

Biographical Sketch of Eugene O'Neill (1888–1953)

'Some day James O'Neill will best be known as the father of
Eugene O'Neill': so Eugene himself frequently boasted
throughout 1912. The claim struck those who heard it not with a
sense of the young man's prescience but of his presumption.
Nothing in his life so far had given any indication that in less
than a decade he would be a playwright to reckon with, shaking
up the American theatre and shaping a new American drama.
Instead, he seemed more likely to become one of the pipe-
dreamers who eternally inhabit Harry Hope's no-chance saloon in
his own *The Iceman Cometh*.

Born on 16 October 1888, to the respected and accomplished
actor James O'Neill and his wife Ella Quinlan O'Neill, Eugene
was to find his family an overwhelming force in his life and to
make it the almost constant subject of his plays. He was the
O'Neills' third son: the eldest, Jamie, had been born ten years
before; a second son, Edmund, had followed five years later. Life
was not easy for the O'Neills and their two young children; James
was already touring the country in *Monte Cristo*, the vehicle that
would spell both his financial success and his artistic defeat (he
succumbed to popular demand and played the role 4000 times
between 1883 and 1912). Ella, convent-educated and proper,
loved her husband but felt she had married beneath her; she
never took to James's theatrical life or to his theatrical friends.
However, the couple could not bear to be parted, and Ella, with
great reluctance, frequently left the children in the care of her
mother to join her husband on the road. Early in 1885, on one of
these occasions, Jamie contracted measles and disobeyed
instructions to stay away from his brother; Edmund became ill
and died.

Such family history might in another case seem irrelevant, but
it is crucial for an understanding of Eugene O'Neill and of his
work. Ella did not want any more children after Edmund's death,
but James, convinced that it would help solace her, persuaded
her to have another. The result was a family tragedy that
blighted all four lives, and not least the new baby, Eugene. In an
attempt to counteract the pain of an exceedingly difficult birth,
Ella was unwittingly precipitated into the morphine addiction

from which she would suffer for the next twenty-six years. James, Jamie, and Eugene were greatly affected by Ella's distraction and withdrawal from reality, but Jamie and Eugene endured a private hell of guilt: Jamie for inadvertently killing the brother whose loss had had such drastic consequences, and Eugene for having been born at all.

Fifteen when he learned of his mother's addiction, Eugene no longer had to fear the mental illness he had up till then suspected he would inherit; the truth, however, was worse. Although summers were spent at the family's home in New London, Connecticut, their haphazard existence in a succession of hotels while James was on tour had already given Eugene a sense of rootlessness that plagued him all his life. Now, guilty that his birth had effected such misery, he developed a deep sense of unbelonging that at times manifested itself as a death-wish. He rejected his parents' Catholicism and, under Jamie's influence, began to drink and to visit brothels. Both Jamie and Eugene, displacing their anger, blamed their father for their mother's condition, accusing him of hiring a 'quack' to attend Ella at Eugene's birth. In fact, even reputable doctors at that time prescribed morphine, and in doses so low that addiction was by no means inevitable.

Eugene entered Princeton in 1906, but only stayed a year, having spent most of his time drinking, cutting classes, and following his own reading interests. It was at this time that he discovered Nietzsche's *Thus Spake Zarathustra*, which together with the works of Strindberg, became his personal bible. After leaving Princeton, he worked for a short time in a New York office job arranged by his father. In the city's Greenwich Village, Hell's Kitchen, and Tenderloin districts, he began to frequent the dives he would immortalise in many of his plays and also began to write poetry. O'Neill remained a heavy drinker for years, though he never drank while writing; in 1926 he gave up alcohol completely, lapsing only a few times thereafter.

Wishing to escape from a romantic entanglement with Kathleen Jenkins, O'Neill let his father arrange for him to join a mining expedition in Honduras in October 1909. Nevertheless, because Kathleen was pregnant, he agreed to marry her shortly before his departure. Having contracted malaria after a few months in Central America, Eugene returned to the US and, without visiting his wife and new-born son (Eugene O'Neill, Jr.), joined his father's company on tour, checking tickets. Shortly afterwards, in June 1910, O'Neill boarded the *Charles Racine*, a Norwegian windjammer, as a working passenger on its two-month voyage to

Buenos Aires. O'Neill loved the sea – he was throughout his life a keen and able swimmer – and now had the chance to experience a sailing life first-hand; it was an experience he would exploit in many of his early plays.

O'Neill remained in Argentina for several months, occasionally working but mainly living as a down-and-out; he sailed back to New York in March 1911 on the S.S. *Ikala*, this time as a member of the crew. He stayed in New York long enough to arrange for a divorce, living in an alcoholic haze at a downtown bar and flophouse called Jimmy-the-Priest's. In July, he signed onto the S.S. *New York* as an ordinary seaman for its voyage to Southampton; he returned in August on the S.S. *Philadelphia* as an able-bodied seaman, a qualification of which he was to remain proud for the rest of his life. Resuming his destitute way of life at Jimmy-the-Priest's – though he regularly attended the performances of Dublin's Abbey Players, who were visiting New York – O'Neill sank progressively into a depression that in January 1912 culminated in a suicide attempt. When he had sufficiently recovered, he rejoined his father's company for a few months, this time taking on small acting roles.

1912 seemed to mark a watershed in O'Neill's life, as evidenced both by his boasting of future fame and by his setting of many of his most autobiographical plays in that year. Moving to New London, Connecticut, in the summer, he worked as a reporter for the *Telegraph*, continued to write poetry, and developed a mild case of tuberculosis. By the end of the year, he was at the Gaylord Farm Sanatorium, where he was to remain for six months. During that time he decided to become a playwright.

Returning to New London in summer 1913 and boarding with the Rippins, a local family, he began to write one-act plays based on his own experiences. O'Neill's father subsidised their publication as *Thirst and Other One Act Plays* in August 1914, and the following September O'Neill enrolled in Professor George Pierce Baker's famous play-writing course at Harvard. Although he did not particularly distinguish himself in the class, his disdain for easy formulaic success made clear his ambition to be an original dramatist.

After his year at Harvard, O'Neill returned to New York and became somewhat involved in the political and intellectual life of Greenwich Village, frequenting the Golden Swan saloon, familiarly known as the 'Hell Hole'. He submitted some plays to the adventurous Washington Square Players, who had recently formed in reaction to the glib, commercial offerings of Broadway; however, the Players were not so adventurous as to stage any of O'Neill's works.

His first real theatrical opportunity came in June 1916 when he accompanied his friend Terry Carlin to Provincetown, at the tip of Massachusetts's Cape Cod. Then, as now, Provincetown boasted a flourishing artists' colony each summer. The previous year, the writer Susan Glaspell, her husband Jig Cook, and other vacationing Greenwich Village friends had staged an impromptu production, marking the birth of what would become the Provincetown Players. When O'Neill arrived in Provincetown, the group were desperately short of plays for their new season. O'Neill offered them *Bound East for Cardiff*, which premiered on 28 July 1916, the first-ever performance of an O'Neill play. His work with the Players also led to his involvement in Greenwich Village's radical circle, which included John Reed, Louise Bryant, Mabel Dodge, and Floyd Dell, among others.

The Provincetown Players' success was such that in September 1916 they moved operations to Greenwich Village, acquiring a base on Macdougal Street, which at O'Neill's suggestion was named the Playwrights' Theatre. During the group's eight subscription seasons between 1916 and 1922, O'Neill had ample opportunity to experiment without regard to commercial considerations. For example, *The Emperor Jones*, staged by the Provincetown Players in November 1920, not only had an African-American for its protagonist but was also considerably shorter than standard length. Despite its unconventionality, the play marked the group's first popular success: following its scheduled performances at the Playwrights' Theatre, it moved uptown to Broadway for an unlimited run. When the original Provincetown Players disbanded, O'Neill, together with the designer Robert Edmond Jones and the critic-producer Kenneth Macgowan, founded the Experimental Theatre, Inc., in 1923. The triumvirate ran the Playwrights' Theatre, now renamed the Provincetown Playhouse, from 1923–25 and the Greenwich Village Theatre from 1924–26.

The Provincetown Players' success with *The Emperor Jones* was not O'Neill's first theatrical triumph. *Beyond the Horizon*, which opened at the Morosco Theatre on Broadway in February 1920, was greeted by extremely favourable reviews, transferred for an extended run, and brought O'Neill his first Pulitzer Prize (the second drama award in the prize's four year history). This success was quickly followed by another: *Anna Christie* opened in November 1921 and brought him a second Pulitzer. He was to win the award twice more, for *Strange Interlude* in 1928 and posthumously in 1956 for *Long Day's Journey into Night*, a record that has not been matched.

By the time of his early success, O'Neill's personal life had undergone considerable change: married for a second time, to the writer Agnes Boulton, he had become a father again with the birth of Shane Rudraighe O'Neill on 30 October 1919 (his last child, Oona, who later married Charlie Chaplin, was born on 14 May 1925). His father had died in August 1920, having lived long enough to see his younger son succeed; in the year prior to his death, Eugene had finally recognised his father's long-standing forbearance and support and had become friendly with him. Ironically, O'Neill's own neediness so dominated his life that he could never be a father to his own children, who all suffered the neglect for which O'Neill had bitterly and unfairly resented his own father. Eugene Jr. committed suicide at the age of forty, and Shane was for many years a heroin addict.

Within three years of his father's death, O'Neill was the sole survivor of his original family: his mother died of a brain tumour in February 1922, and Jamie had drunk himself to death by November 1923. Their deaths freed O'Neill to explore the dark side of his family life, which he proceeded to do in plays as diverse (and variously successful) as *All God's Chillun Got Wings*, *Dynamo*, *Long Day's Journey Into Night*, and *A Moon for the Misbegotten*. Further change was in store: in 1927 O'Neill left Agnes Boulton for Carlotta Monterey, who became his third wife in July 1929. Misogynist, desirous of a mother, unable to separate love from hate, O'Neill had difficult relationships with women. He found his own guilt at his desertion of Agnes too difficult to deal with, and, as he later did with his children, manufactured grievances against her. His third marriage fulfilled his desire that his wife should be completely dedicated to his own interests, but it was a stormy one with cruelty on both sides.

O'Neill was quintessentially an autobiographical playwright; many of his protagonists are recognisable O'Neill figures, sharing the playwright's own lean build and dark deep-set eyes. All of his experiences found their way onto the stage, from the sea-going life depicted in early one-act plays like *Bound East for Cardiff* to his ambivalence about parenthood in *The First Man* to his Strindbergian view of marital relations in *Welded*. This need to depict, explain, and justify himself had considerable ramifications for his role as a playwright: he could not really regard theatre as the collaborative activity it so patently is. Time and again. O'Neill lamented the process of staging his plays, complaining that the ideal play he had seen in his head never existed in production. Whereas playwrights generally welcome the new life that actors and directors bring to their work, O'Neill saw it as a betrayal. So strongly did he feel this that he virtually never went to any productions of his plays, only attending rehearsals in order to advise and to cut when necessary.

In addition, his personal investment in what he wrote often blinded him to its deficiencies: he could be convinced that inferior works like *Welded*, *Dynamo*, and *Days Without End* were undervalued and misjudged. For example, while *Dynamo* ostensibly focused on the relationship between humankind, machines, and religion, it was really O'Neill's working out of his ambivalent relationship to his mother: small wonder that it made more sense to O'Neill than to the critics. However, at his best, O'Neill was able to transmute his personal experiences into the most powerful of dramas, as he does in works like *Long Day's Journey into Night* and *The Iceman Cometh*.

Although he wrote essentially to please himself and to exorcise his private demons (as early as 1924 he claimed that 'Writing is my vacation from living'), O'Neill was genuinely interested in stretching American drama beyond the narrow confines it had so far inhabited. His experiments were many: trying to make the audience share a character's hallucination in *Where the Cross is Made*, extending the audience's endurance by writing four- and five-hour long plays, using set location schematically in *Beyond the Horizon*, incorporating expressionistic elements in *The Hairy Ape*, masking the characters in *The Great God Brown*, modernising the use of the aside in *Strange Interlude*, developing a modern equivalent for the Greek sense of tragedy in *Desire Under the Elms* and *Mourning Becomes Electra*, creating an ambitious play-cycle detailing a critical history of America through the story of one family in *A Tale of Possessors Self-Dispossessed* (of which only *A Touch of the Poet* was completed to his satisfaction).

Although his achievements won him the Nobel prize for literature in 1936, in the last years of his life O'Neill was something of a has-been. He had suffered for years from a hand tremor, caused by a rare degenerative disease of the cerebellum that attacks the motor system, which made writing increasingly difficult; by 1943, it had become impossible. Since O'Neill had never been able to compose at a typewriter or by dictation, his writing career, apart from some revisions, was effectively over. Furthermore, he was extremely depressed by the Second World War: it made his writing seem of little consequence and the staging of his work even less important and appropriate. Consequently, he refused to authorise productions of new plays; none appeared between *Days Without End* in 1933 and *The Iceman*

Cometh in 1946. When the latter was finally staged, the inadequate production did little to restore interest in O'Neill's work.

Throughout his life, O'Neill had roamed far in search of a home and a sense of belonging: New York, Connecticut, Provincetown, Bermuda, France, Georgia, California. Sometime before his death on 27 November 1953, O'Neill struggled up from his bed to complain 'I knew it, I knew it! Born in a goddam hotel room and dying in a hotel room!' Only with the posthumous revival of *The Iceman Cometh* and the first production of *Long Day's Journey into Night* in 1956 did his reputation, like his life, come full circle.

Christine Dymkowski
Lecturer in Drama and Theatre Studies
Royal Holloway and Bedford New College
University of London

Introduction to the Play

Sometime in the late 1920s, O'Neill made notes for an
autobiographical play, but, as with all his work, he never forced
an idea, allowing it instead to simmer in his unconscious.
Returning to the notes early in June 1939, he wrote a scenario
for *The Iceman Cometh* and the next day began work on what
would become *Long Day's Journey into Night*. Again, he first
prepared a scenario, or outline of the play, characters, and
setting, a habit he had formed in Professor Baker's play-writing
class at Harvard. He worked on the scenario during June and
July, and again in February 1940. In late March, he began the
first act dialogue, but feeling demoralised by the war in Europe,
only worked on it for a fortnight or so. Between July and
September 1940 he finished his first draft and by mid-October
his second. O'Neill then put the play away for several months,
returning to cut, revise, and polish it in March 1941.

Writing the play was emotionally exhausting for O'Neill;
Carlotta Monterey described him as 'tortured' by the experience,
'com[ing] out of his study at the end of a day gaunt and
sometimes weeping' (Sheaffer, *Son and Artist*, p. 505). O'Neill's
successive drafts show that he made the play conform more and
more exactly to his family history. For example, he originally
planned to set it in 1907, but changed it to 1912, the same year
he (like the play's younger son) developed tuberculosis. All the
characters are the ages that their real-life counterparts, James,
Ella, Jamie, and Eugene, were in 1912. Similarly, after several
attempts at various names for the family, he settled for reality
(although known as Ella, Mary Ellen was his mother's given
name). Even the new surname of the family, Tyrone, is a
reference to the territory of the early O'Neills in Ireland.
However, O'Neill made one significant departure in regard to
names, exchanging his own with that of his dead brother
Edmund.

The summer cottage where the action takes place is a replica of
the Monte Cristo cottage in New London, Connecticut, that the
family occupied most summers; O'Neill had previously used the
same setting for *Ah, Wilderness!*, a much rosier version of his
youth. Even the pig farmer and Standard Oil millionaire in

Edmund's Act I anecdote had their counterparts in New London. In fact, the play's correspondence to reality is so exact that it is easier to document where *Long Day's Journey* departs from it.

In many ways, O'Neill paints a gloomier picture than biography warrants. Though his father was genuinely careful with money, a result of the childhood deprivations that Tyrone details in the play, he was not so miserly as his counterpart. Whether he employed a cheap doctor to attend Ella at Eugene's birth is questionable: he certainly spent generously on luxuries for his wife, as well on his sons' education. Indeed, there is no suggestion in the play that the father had helped to finance Edmund's trips abroad, as James had done Eugene's. However, O'Neill did spend two days in a state-run tuberculosis sanatorium before his admission to a heavily subsidised private institution. Further, O'Neill suggests that Mary Tyrone will remain a hopeless morphine addict all her life; in fact, Ella was completely cured in 1914. O'Neill regarded this change with some ambivalence: if his mother had finally managed to overcome her habit after twenty-six years, why had she not managed it earlier and saved her son from the miserable guilt of his birth? Finally, Edmund is a rather sanitised version of O'Neill: there is no mention that he had abandoned a wife and child by this time in his life.

When O'Neill finished the play, he deposited it with his publisher, Bennett Cerf of Random House, with the stipulation that it should not be published until twenty-five years after his death and that it should never be produced. His embargo on publication was presumably made to protect the feelings of any surviving relatives. However, in 1955, two years after O'Neill's death, his widow, Carlotta Monterey, the sole executor of his literary estate, instructed Random House to publish the manuscript. Cerf refused, in deference to O'Neill's instructions, which had been repeated as late as 1951. Monterey insisted that O'Neill had only agreed to delay publication at the request of his eldest son; the latter's suicide in 1950 had thus rendered his intention null and void. When Random House still refused to publish the text, Monterey rescinded its rights and assigned them to Yale University Press. The play was published in February 1956 and in the same month performed for the first time (in Swedish) at the Royal Dramatic Theatre in Stockholm. Notices in both the *New York Herald Tribune* and the *New York Times* explain that the play was being staged in Sweden in response to a death-bed request by the playwright.

Evidence exists that O'Neill did consider the play's production

at some point in its composition, since his notes on the play
include some computations about its length. However, that this
was done at an early stage in the writing, before he began on the
dialogue, seems evident from the figures: O'Neill estimates a
running time of 131 minutes for what eventually became a four-
hour play. (He outlined both a five and a four act version with
respective timings of 22, 12, 17, 20, 30 and of 22, 29, 20, 30
minutes.) Such evidence does not in itself cast doubt on O'Neill's
eventual decision to ban production of the play. Indeed, the fact
that Monterey used two different justifications for ignoring her
husband's request suggests that he had not changed his mind
about its being staged.

The Stockholm premiere on 10 February 1956 was, according
to the *New York Times* correspondent Felix Belair Jr., an
'unparallelled success' (11 February 1956, p. 12). The theatre's
director, Karl Ragner Gierow, was a great admirer of O'Neill who
had already staged many other of his plays; indeed, Belair goes
so far as to say that more O'Neill plays had been produced in
Stockholm than anywhere else. Gierow had apparently enlisted
the assistance of United Nations secretary general Dag
Hammarskjöld to secure performing rights. The production
certainly received careful attention: rehearsals had started in mid-
December for what would become a four-and-a-half-hour
emotional marathon for actors and audience alike. The cast,
directed by Bengt Ekerot, consisted of Lars Hanson (Tyrone),
Inga Tidblad (Mary), Ulf Palme (Jamie), and Jarl Kulle
(Edmund). Harry Heintzen, writing in the *New York Herald
Tribune* (11 February 1956, p. 6), reports that the play was
greeted by 'almost unprecedented ovations' with the cast being
cheered for nearly thirty minutes.

Following the success of the play in Sweden, American
producers were naturally anxious to stage it. Monterey decided to
entrust it to José Quintero, whose 1956 revival of *The Iceman
Cometh* had done much to restore O'Neill's reputation. *Long Day's
Journey into Night*, with a running time of three and three-quarter
hours, opened at the Helen Hayes Theatre in New York on 7
November 1956, with Fredric March as Tyrone, Florence
Eldridge as Mary, Jason Robards Jr. as Jamie, and Bradford
Dillman as Edmund. It was a resounding success, going on to
play for 390 performances; in 1957 it won the New York Drama
Critics' Circle Award for the Best American Play, the Tony
Award for Best Play (Fredric March was also named Best Actor),
and the Pulitzer Prize for Drama.

Opening-night critics hailed it as a landmark in American

drama. Brooks Atkinson, writing in the *New York Times* (8 November 1956, p. 47), announced that with its production the American theatre had acquired 'size and stature': a play 'worth waiting for', it had 'restore[d] the drama to literature and the theatre to art'. Walter Kerr, in the *New York Herald Tribune* (8 November 1956, p. 20), considered the play an obligation 'For any one who cares about the American theatre' but also enthused that it was 'a stunning theatrical experience'. Although some critics felt that the play could profitably be trimmed, this reservation was on the whole a minor one and did not mute general praise of the play.

According to Atkinson, the drab set, costumes, and lighting reflected the lugubrious mood of the play. By all accounts, the acting was superb, March's 'masterly' portrayal of Tyrone marking a 'milestone in O'Neill performance' in Atkinson's view. Richard P. Cooke, reviewing the play for the *Wall Street Journal* (9 November 1956, p. 10), regarded Eldridge's performance as the best of her career and described Robards's final speech as a 'small tour-de-force, stirring the tragedy-stilled audience to applause'. The role of Edmund received little critical attention, perhaps reflecting the weakness inherent in the part: many O'Neill scholars have commented on the playwright's rather hazy portrayal of himself. Judith Barlow (*Final Acts*, pp. 110–11) interestingly points out that Robards was originally asked to play Edmund but, sensing the greater dramatic potential in Jamie, opted for that part instead.

Atkinson's view that *Long Day's Journey into Night* really 'comes alive' in the theatre was not a perception shared by British reviewers when the play was first seen here. Again directed by José Quintero, but with a British cast that included Anthony Quayle and Gwen Ffrangçon-Davies as the parents and Ian Bannen and Alan Bates as the elder and younger sons, the play premiered on 8 September 1958 at the Lyceum Theatre, Edinburgh, as part of the Edinburgh Festival; the production shortly moved to the Globe in London, opening on 24 September. W.A. Darlington, writing in the *Daily Telegraph* (25 September 1958, p. 10), found the play 'big but dreary'; he had been impressed in reading it but found its long speeches and lack of narrative drive distracting in the theatre. The reviewer in *The Times* agreed that the 'theatrical effect [was] curiously unsatisfying' (9 September 1958, p. 5); although a bold experiment, the personal facts on which it was based were more moving than the play. Philip Hope-Wallace of the *Guardian* (9 September 1958, p. 5) regarded *Long's Day Journey* as a 'monument of some kind' but implied it was somewhat 'hollow'; it 'earn[ed] its time on the stage' but did not achieve a tragic sense of wonder or elation. Part of the problem, he felt, was the casting of British actors in an American play with a consequent lack of identification with the characters; this in turn led to a loss of humour making the production more portentous than it should have been. His sense that O'Neill just misses in his attempt to create 'really tragic figures' may also betray British uneasiness, perhaps even impatience, at the playwright's wallowing in past and private misery. Darlington hinted at this in complaining that the characters' 'helplessness' makes the play dreary, while *The Times* forthrightly condemned the 'spinelessness' of the Tyrones in both reviews (9 and 25 September 1958).

Some critics were much more enthusiastic, notably Kenneth Tynan, reviewing the London production for the *Observer* (28 September 1958, p. 19). He acknowledged that O'Neill had defects which would 'annihilate most other playwrights' but insisted that 'his strength lies elsewhere', in the personal cost of writing what he felt compelled to. Indeed, his praise is more for the person than the play, as his final words make clear: 'One goes expecting to hear a playwright, and one meets a man'. Norman Shrapnel, reviewing the London production for the *Guardian* (26 September 1958, p. 5), felt that the play had the 'sort of stature' that demanded a wide audience; like classical tragedy, its vision appalled rather than reconciled one to life. Nevertheless, he also described the play as 'hard and heavy going' with 'Flat naturalistic dialogue'.

Tynan indicated that the production was shorter than those he had seen in Berlin and New York, with about a quarter of the text cut. Harold Hobson's review in the *Sunday Times* (28 September 1958, p. 19) reveals that the play was staged in three acts. Many of the cuts appear to have been made after the Edinburgh opening. For example, Darlington's review of the play after it moved to London was much less critical: cuts had been made, the performances had pulled together, and the 'force of character-drawing balance[d] the lack of a dramatic theme' (*Daily Telegraph*, 25 September 1958, p. 10). The acting was widely admired, but Gwen Ffrangçon-Davies received the greatest praise for her portrayal of Mary Tyrone; by all accounts her performance was 'magnificent' (Tynan's judgement).

The first British revival was by the National Theatre on 21 December 1971, with Michael Blakemore directing and Laurence Olivier as Tyrone; Constance Cummings played Mary, Denis Quilley Jamie, and Ronald Pickup Edmund. The play was now hailed as an 'unequivocal masterpiece' (Michael Billington in the *Guardian*, 22 December 1971, p. 8), 'the greatest play to come out of America' (Irving Wardle in *The Times*, 22 December 1971, p. 8), and 'The only major tragedy to come out of America' (John Barber in the *Daily Telegraph*, 22 December 1971, p. 7). Given the four-hour running-time, the play seems to have been given complete; Barber called it 'finely-paced', and Wardle felt the time pass 'in a flash'. Billington's review reveals that the production began with a feeling of 'low-key family amiability', with cracks in the surface only gradually being revealed; the portentousness complained of in the 1958 production seems to have been avoided.

Although the reviews are almost universally admiring, particularly of Olivier's performance, Frank Marcus in the *Sunday Telegraph* (2 January 1972, p. 16) sounded an interesting note of caution: Blakemore, he says, occasionally writes the characters off as 'being Irish' and allowed Olivier's performance to come 'dangerously near to comedy'. John Barber had obviously succumbed to Blakemore's direction: he saw the play as a 'tragedy of all the Irish', of 'a people burdened by a Faith they cannot live up to, locked into the adored, hated, inescapable family, and finding relief only in pouring out home truths and pouring down the hard stuff'. It is tempting to suppose that the distancing effect of the 'Irishness' in this production helped its British audience accept the 'spineless' characters who had so disturbed reviewers of the 1958 production. But such stereotypical portrayal is certainly different from the 'Irish authenticity' that has established the play as a firm favourite in the Republic of Ireland (Shaughnessy, *Eugene O'Neill in Ireland*, p. 71).

The theatrical reception of *Long Day's Journey into Night* points to the difficulties of conclusions based on a mere reading of the text. O'Neill claimed to have written the play 'with deep pity and understanding and forgiveness for *all* the four haunted Tyrones'. Different performances, productions, and audiences have taken their own view: the play is full of defeated but enduring love or is cold and empty; it is the laying bare of private sorrow or an understanding depiction of wider concerns. Some commentators have seen the play as Tyrone's, as O'Neill working out his disapproval of and disappointment in his father and finally presenting him in a sympathetic light; Mary, in this view, remains unredeemed, locked in self-pity. Bravura performances like Olivier's can certainly elicit such response; his two acrobatic descents from the table, teetering deliberately on the edge as he reached for the chandelier's lightbulbs, were greeted with storms of applause. But reviewing this 1971 production, Irving Wardle felt that Mary's is the key part, 'To the extent that the character undergoes the greatest change and exercises the greatest effect on the rest of the family'. His predecessor at *The Times*, reviewing the 1958 production in Edinburgh, vividly described the 'terrifying apparition of the mother', as she speaks her final speech 'deep in morphine': 'every layer of her life is lifted until she is revealed as an unspoiled girl waiting to marry the handsome actor whose incurable meanness is to be her moral ruin'. He judged this scene 'a fine climax', the only time O'Neill's 'memories are absorbed completely in his dramatic imagining'. Whatever O'Neill would have made of these other judgements, he would have appreciated this validation of his own view that the final scene of *Long Day's Journey into Night* was the finest he had ever written.

Christine Dymkowski
February 1991

Sources

Barlow, Judith E. *Final Acts: The Creation of Three Late O'Neill Plays.* Athens: University of Georgia Press, 1985.

Bogard, Travis. *Contour in Time: The Plays of Eugene O'Neill.* Revised ed. New York: Oxford University Press, 1988.

Cargill, Oscar, et al., eds. *O'Neill and His Plays: Four Decades of Criticism.* New York: New York University Press, 1961.

Floyd, Virginia, ed. *Eugene O'Neill at Work: Newly Released Ideas for Plays.* New York: Frederick Ungar, 1981.

Gelb, Arthur and Barbara. *O'Neill.* New York: Harper, 1960.

Miller, Jordan Y. *Eugene O'Neill and the American Critic: A Summary and Bibliographical Checklist.* Second edition, revised. Hamden, Connecticut: Archon, 1973.

Ranald, Margaret Loftus. *The Eugene O'Neill Companion.* Westport, Conn., and London: Greenwood, 1984.

Shaughnessy, Edward L. *Eugene O'Neill in Ireland: The Critical Reception.* New York, London & Westport, Conn: Greenwood, 1988.

Sheaffer, Louis. *O'Neill: Son and Playwright.* London: Dent, 1968.

—————. *O'Neill: Son and Artist.* London: Paul Elek, 1973.

I would also like to thank Sue Cusworth, David Ward of RHBNC Library, and Alex Wilbraham of the National Theatre for help in tracing British productions of O'Neill's plays.

List of O'Neill's Produced Plays

Title	Year Written*	First Production	First London Production
The Web	1913–14	39th Street Theatre, New York 17 March 1924	
Thirst	1913–14	Wharf Theatre, Provincetown, Mass. Summer 1916	
Fog	1913–14	Playwrights' Theater, New York 5 January 1917	
Bound East for Cardiff	1913–14	Wharf Theatre, Provincetown, Mass. 28 July 1916	
Servitude	1913–14	Skylark Theatre N.Y. International Airport 22 April 1960	
Abortion	1913–14	Key Theatre, New York 27 October 1959	
The Movie Man	1914	Key Theatre, New York 27 October 1959	

Title	Year Written*	First Production	First London Production
The Sniper	1915	Playwright's Theater, New York 16 February 1917	(produced at Old Red Lion, Stratford-upon-Avon 27 October 1975)
Before Breakfast	1916	Playwrights' Theater, New York 1 December 1916	
Ile	1916–17	Playwrights' Theater, New York 30 November 1917	Everyman Theatre 17 April 1922
In the Zone	1916–17	Comedy Theater, New York (Washington Square Players) 31 October 1917	Everyman Theatre 15 June 1921
The Long Voyage Home	1916–17	Playwrights' Theater, New York 2 November 1917	Everyman Theatre 12 June 1925
The Moon of The Caribbees	1916–17	Playwrights' Theater, New York 20 December 1918	

S.S. Glencairn (*Bound East for Cardiff*, *In the Zone*, *Moon of the* *Caribbees*, and *Long* *Voyage Home*)		Barnstormer's Barn Provincetown, Massachusetts 14 August 1924	1st performance unknown; revived at Mercury Theatre 9 June 1947
The Rope	1918	Playwrights' Theater, New York 26 April 1918	
The Dreamy Kid	1918	Playwrights' Theater, New York 31 October 1919	
Beyond the Horizon	1918	Morosco Theater, New York 3 February 1920	Regent Theatre (The Repertory Players) 31 January 1926
Where the Cross is Made	1918	Playwrights' Theater, New York 22 November 1918	Arts Theatre 27 October 1927
The Straw	1918–19	Greenwich Village Theater, New York 10 November 1921 (after an out-of-town try-out)	
Exorcism	1919	Playwrights' Theater, New York 26 March 1920	
Chris (1st version of *Anna Christie*)	1919	Apollo Theater, Atlantic City, N.J. 8 March 1920	

Title	Year Written*	First Production	First London Production
Gold	1920	Frazee Theater, New York 1 June 1921	
Anna Christie	1920	Vanderbilt Theater, New York 2 November 1921	Strand Theatre 10 April 1923
The Emperor Jones	1920	Playwrights' Theater, New York 1 November 1920	Ambassadors' Theatre 10 September 1925
Diff'rent	1920	Playwrights' Theater, New York 27 December 1920	Everyman Theatre 4 October 1921
The First Man	1921	Neighborhood Playhouse, New York 4 March 1922	
The Hairy Ape	1921	Playwrights' Theater, New York 9 March 1922	Gate Theatre 26 January 1928
The Fountain	1921–22	Greenwich Village Theater, New York 10 December 1925	
Welded	1922–23	39th Street Theater, New York 17 March 1924	The Playroom Six 16 February 1928

All God's Chillun Got Wings	1923	Provincetown Playhouse, New York 15 May 1924	Gate Theatre 8 November 1926
The Ancient Mariner (adaptation)	1924	Provincetown Playhouse (previously Playwrights' Theater), New York 6 April 1924	
Desire Under The Elms	1924	Greenwich Village Theater, New York 11 November 1924	Gate Theatre 24 February 1931
Marco Millions	1923–25	Guild Theater, New York 9 January 1928	Westminster Theatre 26 December 1938 (also produced at Cambridge Festival, 1932)
The Great God Brown	1925	Greenwich Village Theater, New York 23 January 1926	Strand Theatre (Stage Society) 19 June 1927
Lazarus Laughed	1925–26	Pasadena Community Playhouse, California 9 April 1928	
Strange Interlude	1926–27	John Golden Theater, New York 30 January 1928	Lyric Theatre 3 February 1931

Title	Year Written*	First Production	First London Production
Dynamo	1928	Martin Beck Theater, New York 11 February 1929	
Mourning Becomes Electra	1929–31	Guild Theater, New York 26 October 1931	Westminster Theatre 19 November 1937
Ah, Wilderness!	1932	Nixon Theater, Pittsburgh, Pennsylvania 25 September 1933 (out-of-town tryout before New York opening at Guild Theater, 2 October 1933)	Westminster Theatre 4 May 1936
Days Without End	1932–33	Plymouth Theater, Boston, Mass. 27 December 1933 (out-of-town tryout before New York opening at Guild Theater, 8 January 1934)	Grafton Theatre (Stage Society) 3 Feburary 1935
A Touch of the Poet	1935–42	Royal Dramatic Theatre, Stockholm, Sweden 29 March 1957 (first American production at Helen Hayes Theater, New York, 2 October 1958)	Young Vic Theatre 20 January 1988 (also produced at Ashcroft Theatre, Croydon, 16 September 1963)

More Stately Mansions	1936–42	Royal Dramatic Theatre, Stockholm, Sweden 11 September 1962 (first American production at Ahmanson Theater, Los Angeles, California, 12 November 1967)	Greenwich Theatre 19 September 1974
The Iceman Cometh	1939	Martin Beck Theater, New York 9 October 1946	Arts Theatre 29 January 1958
Long Day's Journey into Night	1939–41	Royal Dramatic Theatre, Stockholm, Sweden 10 February 1956 (first American production at Helen Hayes Theater, New York, 7 November 1956)	Globe Theatre 24 September 1958 (transfer from Lyceum Theatre, Edinburgh, 8 September 1958)
Hughie	1941–42	Royal Dramatic Theatre, Stockholm, Sweden 18 September 1958	Duchess Theatre 18 June 1963
A Moon for the Misbegotten	1943	Hartman Theater, Columbus, Ohio (Guild Theater production) 20 February 1947	Arts Theatre 20 January 1960

*Dates of composition are approximate.

LONG DAY'S JOURNEY
INTO NIGHT

For Carlotta, on our 12th Wedding Anniversary

Dearest: I give you the original script of this play of old sorrow, written in tears and blood. A sadly inappropriate gift, it would seem, for a day celebrating happiness. But you will understand. I mean it as a tribute to your love and tenderness which gave me the faith in love that enabled me to face my dead at last and write this play – write it with deep pity and understanding and forgiveness for <u>all</u> the four haunted Tyrones.

These twelve years, Beloved One, have been a Journey into Light – into love. You know my gratitude. And my love!

Gene

Tao House
July 22, 1941

The Royal National Theatre and Bristol Old Vic's co-production of *Long Day's Journey Into Night* opened at the Bristol Old Vic on 19 February 1991 and toured Sheffield, Glasgow, Nottingham, Manchester, Bradford, Newcastle and Cardiff before opening at the National's Lyttelton Theatre on 21 May 1991.
The cast was as follows:-

JAMES TYRONE	Timothy West
MARY CAVAN TYRONE	Prunella Scales
JAMES TYRONE JR.	Sean McGinley
EDMUND TYRONE	Stephen Dillane
CATHLEEN	Geraldine Fitzgerald

Directed by Howard Davies
Designed by John Gunter
Lighting by Mark Henderson
Music by Dominic Muldowney

Characters

JAMES TYRONE
MARY CAVAN TYRONE, his wife
JAMES TYRONE, JR., their elder son
EDMUND TYRONE, their younger son
CATHLEEN, second girl

Scenes

ACT ONE

Living-room of the Tyrones' summer home
8.30 a.m. on a day in August, 1912

ACT TWO

Scene 1: The same, around 12.45
Scene 2: The same, about a half-hour later

ACT THREE

The same, around 6.30 that evening

ACT FOUR

The same, around midnight

ACT ONE

Scene. Living-room of JAMES TYRONE'*s summer home on a morning in August,* 1912.

At rear are two double doorways with portières. The one at right leads into a front parlour with the formally arranged, set appearance of a room rarely occupied. The other opens on a dark, windowless back parlour, never used except as a passage from living-room to dining-room. Against the wall between the doorways is a small bookcase, with a picture of Shakespeare above it, containing novels by Balzac, Zola, Stendhal, philosophical and sociological works by Schopenhauer, Nietzsche, Marx, Engels, Kropotkin, Max Sterner, plays by Ibsen, Shaw, Strindberg, poetry by Swinburne, Rossetti, Wilde, Ernest Dowson, Kipling, etc.

In the right wall, rear, is a screen door leading out on the porch which extends halfway around the house. Farther forward, a series of three windows looks over the front lawn to the harbour and the avenue that runs along the water front. A small wicker table and an ordinary oak desk are against the wall, flanking the windows.

In the left wall, a similar series of windows looks out on the grounds behind the house. Beneath them is a wicker couch with cushions, its head toward rear. Farther back is a large, glassed-in bookcase with sets of Dumas, Victor Hugo, Charles Lever, three sets of Shakespeare, The World's Best Literature in fifty large volumes, Hume's History of England, Thiers' History of the Consulate and Empire, Smollett's History of England, Gibbons Roman Empire and miscellaneous volumes of old plays, poetry, and several histories of Ireland. The astonishing thing about these sets is that all the volumes have the look of having been read and reread.

The hardwood floor is nearly covered by a rug, inoffensive in design and colour. At centre is a round table with a green-shaded reading lamp, the cord plugged in one of the four sockets in the chandelier above. Around the table within reading-light range are four chairs, three of them wicker armchairs, the fourth (at right front of table) a varnished oak rocker with leather bottom.

It is about 8.30. Sunshine comes through the windows at right.

As the curtain rises, the family have just finished breakfast. MARY TYRONE *and her husband enter together from the back parlour, coming from the dining-room.*

MARY *is fifty-four, about medium height. She still has a young, graceful figure, a trifle plump, but showing little evidence of middle-aged waist and hips, although she is not tightly corseted. Her face is distinctly Irish in type. It must once have been extremely pretty, and is still striking. It does not match her healthy figure but is thin and pale with the bone structure prominent. Her nose is long and straight, her mouth wide with full, sensitive lips. She uses no rouge or any sort of make-up. Her high forehead is framed by thick, pure white hair. Accentuated by her pallor and white hair, her dark brown eyes appear black. They are unusually large and beautiful, with black brows and long curling lashes.*

What strikes one immediately is her extreme nervousness. Her hands are never still. They were once beautiful hands, with long, tapering fingers, but rheumatism has knotted the joints and warped the fingers, so that they now have an ugly crippled look. One avoids looking at them, the more so because one is conscious she is sensitive about their appearance and humiliated by her inability to control the nervousness which draws attention to them.

She is dressed simply but with a sure sense of what becomes her. Her hair is arranged with fastidious care. Her voice is soft and attractive. When she is merry, there is a touch of Irish lilt in it.

Her most appealing quality is the simple, unaffected charm of a shy convent-girl youthfulness she has never lost − an innate unwordly innocence.

JAMES TYRONE *is sixty-five but looks ten years younger. About five feet eight, broad-shouldered and deep-chested, he seems taller and slenderer because of his bearing, which has a soldierly quality of head up, chest out, stomach in, shoulders squared. His face has begun to break down but he is still remarkably good-looking − a big, finely shaped head, a handsome profile, deep-set light-brown eyes. His grey hair is thin with a bald spot like a monk's tonsure.*

The stamp of his profession is unmistakably on him. Not that he indulges in any of the deliberate temperamental posturings of the stage star. He is by nature and preference a simple, unpretentious man, whose inclinations are still close to his humble beginnings and his Irish farmer forebears. But the actor shows in all his unconscious habits of speech, movement and gesture. These have the quality of belonging to a studied technique. His voice is remarkably fine, resonant and flexible, and he takes great pride in it.

His clothes, assuredly, do not costume any romantic part. He wears a threadbare, ready-made, grey sack suit and shineless black shoes, a collarless shirt with a thick white handkerchief knotted loosely around his throat.

There is nothing picturesquely careless about this get-up. It is commonplace shabby. He believes in wearing his clothes to the limit of usefulness, is dressed now for gardening, and doesn't give a damn how he looks.

He has never been really sick a day in his life. He has no nerves. There is a lot of stolid, earthy peasant in him, mixed with streaks of sentimental melancholy and rare flashes of intuitive sensibility.

TYRONE's arm is around his wife's waist as they appear from the back parlour. Entering the living-room he gives her a playful hug.

TYRONE. You're a fine armful now, Mary, with those twenty pounds you've gained.

MARY (*smiles affectionately*). I've gotten too fat, you mean, dear. I really ought to reduce.

TYRONE. None of that, my lady! You're just right. We'll have no talk of reducing. Is that why you ate so little breakfast?

MARY. So little? I thought I ate a lot.

TYRONE. You didn't. Not as much as I'd like to see, anyway.

MARY (*teasingly*). Oh you! You expect everyone to eat the enormous breakfast you do. No one else in the world could without dying of indigestion. (*She comes forward to stand by the right of table.*)

TYRONE (*following her*). I hope I'm not as big a glutton as that sounds. (*With hearty satisfaction.*) But thank God, I've kept my appetite and I've the digestion of a young man of twenty, if I am sixty-five.

MARY. You surely have, James. No one could deny that.

She laughs and sits in the wicker armchair at right rear of table. He comes around behind her and selects a cigar from a box on the table and cuts off the end with a little clipper. From the dining-room JAMIE's and EDMUND's voices are heard. MARY turns her head that way.

Why did the boys stay in the dining-room, I wonder? Cathleen must be waiting to clear the table.

TYRONE (*jokingly but with an undercurrent of resentment*). It's a secret confab they don't want me to hear, I suppose. I'll bet they're cooking up some new scheme to touch the Old Man.

She is silent on this, keeping her head turned toward their voices. Her hands appear on the table top, moving restlessly. He lights his cigar and sits down in the rocker at the right of table, which is his chair, and puffs contentedly.

There's nothing like the first after-breakfast cigar, if it's a good one, and this new lot have the right mellow flavour. They're a great bargain, too. I got them dead cheap. It was McGuire put me on to them.

MARY (*a trifle acidly*). I hope he didn't put you on to any new piece of property at the same time. His real-estate bargains don't work out so well.

TYRONE (*defensively*). I wouldn't say that, Mary. After all, he was the one who advised me to buy that place on Chestnut Street and I made a quick turnover on it for a fine profit.

MARY (*smiles now with teasing affection*). I know. The famous one stroke of good luck. I'm sure McGuire never dreamed – (*Then she pats his hand.*) Never mind, James. I know it's a waste of breath trying to convince you you're not a cunning real-estate speculator.

TYRONE (*huffily*). I've no such idea. But land is land, and it's safer than the stocks and bonds of Wall Street swindlers. (*Then placatingly.*) But let's not argue about business this early in the morning.

A pause. The boys' voices are again heard and one of them has a fit of coughing. MARY listens worriedly. Her fingers play nervously on the table top.

MARY. James, it's Edmund you ought to scold for not eating enough. He hardly touched anything except coffee. He needs to eat to keep up his strength. I keep telling him that but he says he simply has no appetite. Of course, there's nothing takes away your appetite like a bad summer cold.

TYRONE. Yes, it's only natural. So don't let yourself get worried –

MARY (*quickly*). Oh, I'm not. I know he'll be all right in a few days if he takes care of himself. (*As if she wanted to dismiss the subject but can't.*) But it does seem a shame he should have to be sick right now.

TYRONE. Yes, it is bad luck. (*He gives her a quick, worried look.*) But you mustn't let it upset you, Mary. Remember, you've got to take care of yourself, too.

MARY (*quickly*). I'm not upset. There's nothing to be upset about. What makes you think I'm upset?

TYRONE. Why, nothing, except you've seemed a bit high-strung the past few days.

MARY (*forcing a smile*). I have? Nonsense, dear. It's your imagination. (*With sudden tenseness*). You really must not watch me all the time, James. I mean, it makes me self-conscious.

TYRONE (*putting a hand over one of her nervously playing ones*). Now, now, Mary. That's your imagination. If I've watched you it was to admire how fat and beautiful you looked. (*His voice is suddenly moved by deep feeling.*) I can't tell you the deep happiness it gives me, darling, to see you as you've been since you came back to us, your dear old self again. (*He leans over and kisses her cheek impulsively – then turning back adds with a constrained air.*) So keep up the good work, Mary.

MARY (*has turned her head away*). I will, dear. (*She gets up restlessly and goes to the windows at right.*) Thank heavens, the fog is gone. (*She turns back.*) I do feel out of sorts this morning. I wasn't able to get much sleep with that awful foghorn going all night long.

TYRONE. Yes, it's like having a sick whale in the back yard. It kept me awake, too.

MARY (*affectionately amused*). Did it? You had a strange way of showing your restlessness. You were snoring so hard I couldn't tell which was the foghorn! (*She comes to him, laughing, and pats his cheek playfully.*) Ten foghorns couldn't disturb you. You haven't a nerve in you. You've never had.

TYRONE (*his vanity piqued – testily*). Nonsense. You always exaggerate about my snoring.

MARY. I couldn't. If you could only hear yourself once –

A burst of laughter comes from the dining-room. She turns her head, smiling.

What's the joke, I wonder?

TYRONE (*grumpily*). It's on me. I'll bet that much. It's always on the Old Man.

MARY (*teasingly*). Yes, it's terrible the way we all pick on you, isn't it? You're so abused! (*She laughs – then with a pleased, relieved air.*) Well, no matter what the joke is about, it's a relief to hear Edmund laugh. He's been so down in the mouth lately.

TYRONE (*ignoring this – resentfully*). Some joke of Jamie's, I'll wager. He's for ever making sneering fun of somebody, that one.

MARY. Now don't start in on poor Jamie, dear. (*Without conviction.*) He'll turn out all right in the end, you wait and see.

TYRONE. He'd better start soon, then. He's nearly thirty-four.

MARY (*ignoring this*). Good heavens, are they going to stay in the dining-room all day? (*She goes to the back parlour doorway and calls.*) Jamie! Edmund! Come in the living-room and give Cathleen a chance to clear the table.

EDMUND *calls back,* 'We're coming, Mama.' *She goes back to the table.*

TYRONE (*grumbling*). You'd find excuses for him no matter what he did.

MARY (*sitting down beside him, pats his hand*). Shush.

Their sons JAMES JR. and EDMUND enter together from the back parlour. They are both grinning, still chuckling over what had caused their laughter, and as they come forward they glance at their father and their grins grow broader.

JAMIE, the elder, is thirty-three. He has his father's broad-shouldered, deep-chested physique, is an inch taller and weighs less, but appears shorter and stouter because he lacks TYRONE's bearing and graceful carriage. He also lacks his father's vitality.

The signs of premature disintegration are on him. His face is still good-looking, despite marks of dissipation, but it has never been handsome like TYRONE's, although JAMIE resembles him rather than his mother. He has fine brown eyes, their colour midway between his father's lighter and his mother's darker ones. His hair is thinning and already there is indication of a bald spot like TYRONE's. His nose is unlike that of any other member of the family, pronouncedly aquiline. Combined with his habitual expression of cynicism it gives his countenance a Mephistophelian cast. But on the rare occasions when he smiles without sneering, his personality possesses the remnant of a humorous, romantic, irresponsible Irish charm – that of the beguiling ne'er-do-well, with a strain of the sentimentally poetic, attractive to women and popular with men.

He is dressed in an old sack suit, not as shabby as TYRONE's, and wears a collar and tie. His fair skin is sunburned a reddish, freckled tan.

EDMUND *is ten years younger than his brother, a couple of inches taller, thin and wiry. Where* JAMIE *takes after his father, with little resemblance to his mother,* EDMUND *looks like both his parents, but is more like his mother. Her big, dark eyes are the dominant feature in his long, narrow Irish face. His mouth has the same quality of hypersensitiveness hers possesses. His high forehead is hers accentuated, with dark brown hair, sunbleached to red at the ends, brushed straight back from it. But his nose, is his father's, and his face in profile recalls* TYRONE's. EDMUND's *hands are noticeably like his mother's, with the same exceptionally long fingers. They even have to a minor degree the same nervousness. It is in the quality of extreme nervous sensibility that the likeness of* EDMUND *to his mother is most marked.*

He is plainly in bad health. Much thinner than he should be, his eyes appear feverish and his cheeks are sunken. His skin, in spite of being sunburned a deep brown, has a parched sallowness. He wears a shirt, collar and tie, no coat, old flannel trousers, brown sneakers.

MARY (*turns smilingly to them, in a merry tone that is a bit forced*). I've been teasing your father about his snoring. (*To* TYRONE.) I'll leave it to the boys, James. They must have heard you. No, not you, Jamie. I could hear you down the hall almost as bad as your father. You're like him. As soon as your head touches the pillow you're off and ten foghorns couldn't wake you. (*She stops abruptly, catching* JAMIE's *eyes regarding her with an uneasy, probing look. Her smile vanishes and her manner becomes self-conscious.*) Why are you staring, Jamie? (*Her hands flutter up to her hair.*) Is my hair coming down? It's hard for me to do it up properly now. My eyes are getting so bad and I never can find my glasses.

JAMIE (*looks away guiltily*). Your hair's all right, Mama. I was only thinking how well you look.

TYRONE (*heartily*). Just what I've been telling her, Jamie. She's so fat and sassy, there'll soon be no holding her.

EDMUND. Yes, you certainly look grand, Mama.

She is reassured and smiles at him lovingly. He winks with a kidding grin.

I'll back you up about Papa's snoring. Gosh, what a racket!

JAMIE. I heard him, too. (*He quotes, putting on a ham-actor manner.*) 'The Moor, I know his trumpet.'

His mother and brother laugh.

TYRONE (*scathingly*). If it takes my snoring to make you remember Shakespeare instead of the dope sheet on the ponies, I hope I'll keep on with it.

MARY. Now, James! You mustn't be so touchy.

JAMIE *shrugs his shoulders and sits down in the chair on her right.*

EDMUND (*irritably*). Yes, for Pete's sake, Papa! The first thing after breakfast! Give it a rest, can't you?

He slumps down in the chair at left of table next to his brother. His father ignores him.

MARY (*reprovingly*). Your father wasn't finding fault with you. You don't have to always take Jamie's part. You'd think you were the one ten years older.

JAMIE (*boredly*). What's all the fuss about? Let's forget it.

TYRONE (*contemptuously*). Yes, forget! Forget everything and face nothing! It's a convenient philosophy if you've no ambition in life except to –

MARY. James, do be quiet. (*She puts an arm around his shoulder – coaxingly.*) You must have gotten out of the wrong side of the bed this morning. (*To the boys, changing the subject.*) What were you two grinning about like Cheshire cats when you came in? What was the joke?

TYRONE (*with a painful effort to be a good sport*). Yes, let us in on it, lads. I told your mother I knew damned well it would be one on me, but never mind that, I'm used to it.

JAMIE (*dryly*). Don't look at me. This is the Kid's story.

EDMUND (*grins*). I meant to tell you last night, Papa, and forgot it. Yesterday when I went for a walk I dropped in at the Inn –

MARY (*worriedly*). You shouldn't drink now, Edmund.

EDMUND (*ignoring this*). And who do you think I met there, with a beautiful bun on, but Shaughnessy, the tenant on that farm of yours.

MARY (*smiling*). That dreadful man! But he is funny.

TYRONE (*scowling*). He's not so funny when you're his landlord. He's a wily Shanty Mick, that one. He could hide behind a corkscrew. What's he complaining about now, Edmund – for I'm damned sure he's complaining. I suppose he wants his rent lowered. I let him have the place for almost nothing, just to keep someone on it, and he never pays that till I threaten to evict him.

EDMUND. No, he didn't beef about anything. He was so pleased with life he even bought a drink, and that's practically unheard of. He was delighted because he'd had a fight with your friend, Harker, the Standard Oil millionaire, and won a glorious victory.

MARY (*with amused dismay*). Oh, Lord! James, you'll really have to do something –

TYRONE. Bad luck to Shaughnessy, anyway!

JAMIE (*maliciously*). I'll bet the next time you see Harker at the Club and give him the old respectful bow, he won't see you.

EDMUND. Yes. Harker will think you're no gentleman for harbouring a tenant who isn't humble in the presence of a king of America.

TYRONE. Never mind the Socialist gabble. I don't care to listen –

MARY (*tactfully*). Go on with your story, Edmund.

EDMUND (*grins at his father provocatively*). Well, you remember, Papa, the ice pond on Harker's estate is right next to the farm, and you remember Shaughnessy keeps pigs. Well, it seems there's a break in the fence and the pigs have been bathing in the millionaire's ice pond, and Harker's foreman told him he was sure Shaughnessy had broken the fence on purpose to give his pigs a free wallow.

MARY (*shocked and amused*). Good heavens!

TYRONE (*sourly, but with a trace of admiration*). I'm sure he did, too, the dirty scallywag. It's like him.

EDMUND. So Harker came in person to rebuke Shaughnessy. (*He chuckles.*) A very bonehead play! If I needed any further proof that our ruling plutocrats, especially the ones who inherited their boodle, are not mental giants, that would clinch it.

TYRONE (*with appreciation, before he thinks*). Yes, he'd be no match for Shaughnessy. (*Then he growls.*) Keep your damned anarchist remarks to yourself. I won't have them in my house. (*But he is full of eager anticipation.*) What happened?

EDMUND. Harker had as much chance as I would with Jack Johnson. Shaughnessy got a few drinks under his belt and was waiting at the gate to welcome him. He told me he never gave Harker a chance to open his mouth. He began by shouting that he was no slave Standard Oil could trample on. He was a King of Ireland, if he had his rights, and scum was scum to him, no matter how much money it had stolen from the poor.

MARY. Oh, Lord! (*But she can't help laughing.*)

EDMUND. Then he accused Harker of making his foreman break down the fence to entice the pigs into the ice pond in order to destroy them. The poor pigs, Shaughnessy yelled, had caught their death of cold. Many of them were dying of pneumonia, and several others had been taken down with cholera from drinking the poisoned water. He told Harker he was hiring a lawyer to sue him for damages. And he wound up saying that he had to put up with poison ivy, ticks, potato bugs, snakes and skunks on his farm, but he was an honest man who drew the line somewhere, and he'd be damned if he'd stand for a Standard Oil thief trespassing. So would Harker kindly remove his dirty feet from the premises before he sicked the dog on him. And Harker did!

He and JAMIE *laugh.*

MARY (*shocked but giggling*). Heavens, what a terrible tongue that man has!

TYRONE (*admiringly before he thinks*). The damned old scoundrel! By God, you can't beat him! (*He laughs – then stops abruptly and scowls.*) The dirty blackguard! He'll get me in serious trouble yet. I hope you told him I'd be mad as hell –

EDMUND. I told him you'd be tickled to death over the great Irish victory, and so you are. Stop faking, Papa.

TYRONE. Well, I'm not tickled to death.

MARY (*teasingly*). You are, too, James. You're simply delighted!

TYRONE. No, Mary, a joke is a joke, but –

EDMUND. I told Shaughnessy he should have reminded Harker that a Standard Oil millionaire ought to welcome the flavour of hog in his ice water as an appropriate touch.

TYRONE. The devil you did! (*Frowning.*) Keep your damned Socialist anarchist sentiments out of my affairs!

EDMUND. Shaughnessy almost wept because he hadn't thought of that one, but he said he'd include it in a letter he's writing to Harker, along with a few other insults he'd overlooked.

He and JAMIE *laugh.*

TYRONE. What are you laughing at? There's nothing funny – A fine son you are to help that blackguard get me into a lawsuit!

MARY. Now, James, don't lose your temper.

TYRONE (*turns on* JAMIE). And you're worse than he is, encouraging him. I suppose you're regretting you weren't there to prompt Shaughnessy with a few nastier insults. You've a fine talent for that, if for nothing else.

MARY. James! There's no reason to scold Jamie.

JAMIE *is about to make some sneering remark to his father, but he shrugs his shoulders.*

EDMUND (*with sudden nervous exasperation*). Oh, for God's sake, Papa! If you're starting that stuff again, I'll beat it. (*He jumps up.*) I left my book upstairs, anyway. (*He goes to the front parlour, saying disgustedly:*) God, Papa, I should think you'd get sick of hearing yourself –

He disappears. TYRONE *looks after him angrily.*

MARY. You mustn't mind Edmund, James. Remember he isn't well.

EDMUND *can be heard coughing as he goes upstairs.*

(*She adds nervously.*) A summer cold makes anyone irritable.

JAMIE (*genuinely concerned*). It's not just a cold he's got. The Kid is damned sick.

His father gives him a sharp warning look but he doesn't see it.

MARY (*turns on him resentfully*). Why do you say that? It *is* just a cold! Anyone can tell that! You always imagine things!

TYRONE (*with another warning glance at* JAMIE – *easily*). All Jamie meant was Edmund might have a touch of something else, too, which makes his cold worse.

JAMIE. Sure, Mama. That's all I meant.

TYRONE. Doctor Hardy thinks it might be a bit of malarial fever he caught when he was in the tropics. If it is, quinine will soon cure it.

MARY (*a look of contemptuous hostility flashes across her face*). Doctor Hardy! I wouldn't believe a thing he said, if he swore on a stack of Bibles! I know what doctors are. They're all alike. Anything, they don't care what, to keep you coming to them. (*She stops short, overcome by a fit of acute self-consciousness as she catches their eyes fixed on her. Her hands jerk nervously to her hair. She forces a smile.*) What is it? What are you looking at? Is my hair – ?

TYRONE (*puts his arm around her – with guilty heartiness, giving her a playful hug*). There's nothing wrong with your hair. The healthier and fatter you get, the vainer you become. You'll soon spend half the day primping before the mirror.

MARY (*half reassured*). I really should have new glasses. My eyes are so bad now.

TYRONE (*with Irish blarney*). Your eyes are beautiful, and well you know it.

He gives her a kiss. Her face lights up with a charming, shy embarrassment. Suddenly and startlingly one sees in her face the girl she had once been, not a ghost of the dead, but still a living part of her.

MARY. You mustn't be so silly, James. Right in front of Jamie!

TYRONE. Oh, he's on to you, too. He knows this fuss about eyes and hair is only fishing for compliments. Eh, Jamie?

JAMIE (*his face has cleared, too, and there is an old boyish charm in his loving smile at his mother*). Yes. You can't kid us, Mama.

MARY (*laughs and an Irish lilt comes into her voice*). Go along with both of you! (*Then she speaks with a girlish gravity.*) But I did truly have beautiful hair once, didn't I, James?

TYRONE. The most beautiful in the world!

MARY. It was a rare shade of reddish brown and so long it came down below my knees. You ought to remember it too, Jamie. It wasn't until after Edmund was born that I had a single grey hair. Then it began to turn white. (*The girlishness fades from her face.*)

TYRONE (*quickly*). And that made it prettier than ever.

MARY (*again embarrassed and pleased*). Will you listen to your father, Jamie – after thirty-five years of marriage! He isn't a great actor for nothing, is he? What's come over you, James?

Are you pouring coals of fire on my head for teasing you about snoring? Well then, I take it all back. It must have been only the foghorn I heard. (*She laughs, and they laugh with her. Then she changes to a brisk businesslike air.*) But I can't stay with you any longer, even to hear compliments. I must see the cook about dinner and the day's marketing. (*She gets up and sighs with humorous exaggeration.*) Bridget is so lazy. And so sly. She begins telling me about her relatives so I can't get a word in edgeways and scold her. Well, I might as well get it over. (*She goes to the back-parlour doorway, then turns, her face worried again.*) You mustn't make Edmund work on the grounds with you, James, remember. (*Again with the strange obstinate set to her face.*) Not that he isn't strong enough, but he'd perspire and he might catch more cold.

She disappears through the back parlour. TYRONE *turns on* JAMIE *condemningly.*

TYRONE. You're a fine lunkhead! Haven't you any sense? The one thing to avoid is saying anything that would get her more upset over Edmund.

JAMIE (*shrugging his shoulders*). All right. Have it your way. I think it's the wrong idea to let Mama go on kidding herself. It will only make the shock worse when she has to face it. Anyway, you can see she's deliberately fooling herself with that summer-cold talk. She knows better.

TYRONE. Knows? Nobody knows yet.

JAMIE. Well, I do. I was with Edmund when he went to Doc Hardy on Monday. I heard him pull that touch of malaria stuff. He was stalling. That isn't what he thinks any more. You know it as well as I do. You talked to him when you went uptown yesterday, didn't you?

TYRONE. He couldn't say anything for sure yet. He's to phone me today before Edmund goes to him.

JAMIE (*slowly*). He thinks it's consumption, doesn't he, Papa?

TYRONE (*reluctantly*). He said it might be.

JAMIE (*moved, his love for his brother coming out*). Poor kid! God damn it! (*He turns on his father accusingly.*) It might never have happened if you'd sent him to a real doctor when he first got sick.

TYRONE. What's the matter with Hardy? He's always been our doctor up here.

JAMIE. Everything's the matter with him! Even in this hick burg he's rated third class! He's a cheap old quack!

TYRONE. That's right! Run him down! Run down everybody! Everyone is a fake to you!

JAMIE (*contemptuously*). Hardy only charges a dollar. That's what makes you think he's a fine doctor!

TYRONE (*stung*). That's enough! You're not drunk now! There's no excuse – (*He controls himself – a bit defensively.*) If you mean I can't afford one of the fine society doctors who prey on the rich summer people –

JAMIE. Can't afford? You're one of the biggest property owners around here.

TYRONE. That doesn't mean I'm rich. It's all mortgaged –

JAMIE. Because you always buy more instead of paying off mortgages. If Edmund was a lousy acre of land you wanted, the sky would be the limit!

TYRONE. That's a lie! And your sneers against Doctor Hardy are lies! He doesn't put on frills, or have an office in a fashionable location, or drive around in an expensive automobile. That's what you pay for with those other five-dollars-to-look-at-your-tongue fellows, not their skill.

JAMIE (*with a scornful shrug of his shoulders*). Oh, all right. I'm a fool to argue. You can't change the leopard's spots.

TYRONE (*with rising anger*). No, you can't. You've taught me that lesson only too well. I've lost all hope you will ever change yours. You dare tell me what I can afford? You've never known the value of a dollar and never will! You've never saved a dollar in your life! At the end of each season you're penniless! You've thrown your salary away every week on whores and whiskey!

JAMIE. My salary! Christ!

TYRONE. It's more than you're worth, and you couldn't get that if it wasn't for me. If you weren't my son, there isn't a manager in the business who would give you a part, your reputation stinks so. As it is, I have to humble my pride and beg for you, saying you've turned over a new leaf, although I know it's a lie!

JAMIE. I never wanted to be an actor. You forced me on the stage.

TYRONE. That's a lie! You made no effort to find anything else to do. You left it to me to get you a job and I have no influence except in the theatre. Forced you! You never wanted to do anything except loaf in bar-rooms! You'd have been content to sit back like a lazy lunk and sponge on me for the rest of your life! After all the money I'd wasted on your education, and all you did was get fired in disgrace from every college you went to!

JAMIE. Oh, for God's sake, don't drag up that ancient history!

TYRONE. It's not ancient history that you have to come home every summer to live on me.

JAMIE. I earn my board and lodging working on the grounds. It saves you hiring a man.

TYRONE. Bah! You have to be driven to do even that much! (*His anger ebbs into a weary complaint.*) I wouldn't give a damn if you ever displayed the slightest sign of gratitude. The only thanks is to have you sneer at me for a dirty miser, sneer at my profession, sneer at every damned thing in the world – except yourself.

JAMIE (*wryly*). That's not true, Papa. You can't hear me talking to myself, that's all.

TYRONE (*stares at him puzzledly, then quotes mechanically*). 'Ingratitude, the vilest weed that grows'!

JAMIE. I could see that line coming! God, how many thousand times – ! (*He stops, bored with their quarrel, and shrugs his shoulders.*) All right, Papa, I'm a bum. Anything you like, so long as it stops the argument.

TYRONE (*with indignant appeal now*). If you'd get ambition in your head instead of folly! You're young yet. You could still make your mark. You had the talent to become a fine actor! You have it still. You're my son – !

JAMIE (*boredly*). Let's forget me. I'm not interested in the subject. Neither are you.

TYRONE *gives up.* JAMIE *goes on casually.*

What started us on this? Oh, Doc Hardy. When is he going to call you up about Edmund?

TYRONE. Around lunch time. (*He pauses – then defensively.*) I couldn't have sent Edmund to a better doctor. Hardy's treated him whenever he was sick up here, since he was knee-high. He knows his constitution as no other doctor could. It's not a question of my being miserly, as you'd like to make out. (*Bitterly.*) And what could the finest specialist in America do for Edmund, after he's deliberately ruined his health by the mad life he's led ever since he was fired from college? Even before that, when he was in prep school, he began dissipating and playing the Broadway sport to imitate you, when he's never had your constitution to stand it. You're a healthy hulk like me – or you were at his age – but he's always been a bundle of nerves like his mother. I've warned him for years his body couldn't stand it, but he wouldn't heed me, and now it's too late.

JAMIE (*sharply*). What do you mean, too late? You talk as if you thought –

TYRONE (*guiltily explosive*). Don't be a damned fool! I meant nothing but what's plain to anyone! His health has broken down and he may be an invalid for a long time.

JAMIE (*stares at his father, ignoring his explanation*). I know it's an Irish peasant idea consumption is fatal. It probably is when you live in a hovel on a bog, but over here, with modern treatment –

TYRONE. Don't I know that! What are you gabbing about, anyway? And keep your dirty tongue off Ireland, with your sneers about peasants and bogs and hovels! (*Accusingly.*) The less you say about Edmund's sickness, the better for your conscience! You're more responsible than anyone!

JAMIE (*stung*). That's a lie! I won't stand for that, Papa!

TYRONE. It's the truth! You've been the worst influence for him. He grew up admiring you as a hero! A fine example you set him! If you ever gave him advice except in the ways of rottenness, I've never heard of it! You made him old before his time, pumping him full of what you consider worldly wisdom, when he was too young to see that your mind was so poisoned by your own failure in life, you wanted to believe every man was a knave with his soul for sale, and every woman who wasn't a whore was a fool!

JAMIE. (*with a defensive air of weary indifference again*). All right. I did put Edmund wise to things, but not until I saw he'd started to raise hell, and knew he'd laugh at me if I tried the good advice, older brother stuff. All I did was make a pal of him and be absolutely frank so he'd learn from my mistakes that – (*He *shrugs his shoulders – cynically.*) Well, that if you can't be good you can at least be careful.

His father snorts contemptuously. Suddenly JAMIE *becomes really moved.*

That's a rotten accusation, Papa. You know how much the Kid means to me, and how close we've always been – not like the usual brothers! I'd do anything for him.

TYRONE (*impressed – mollifyingly*). I know you may have thought it was for the best, Jamie. I didn't say you did it deliberately to harm him.

JAMIE. Besides, it's damned rot! I'd like to see anyone influence Edmund more than he wants to be. His quietness fools people into thinking they can do what they like with him. But he's stubborn as hell inside and what he does is what he wants to do, and to hell with anyone else! What had I to do with all the crazy stunts he's pulled in the last few years – working his way over all the map as a sailor and all that stuff. I thought that was a damned fool idea, and I told him so. You can't imagine me getting fun out of being on the beach in South America or living in filthy dives, drinking rotgut, can you? No, thanks! I'll stick to Broadway, and a room with a bath, and bars that serve bonded Bourbon.

TYRONE. You and Broadway! It's made you what you are! (*With a touch of pride.*) Whatever Edmund's done, he's had the guts to go off on his own, where he couldn't come whining to me the minute he was broke.

JAMIE (*stung into sneering jealousy*). He's always come home broke finally, hasn't he? And what did his going away get him? Look at him now! (*He is suddenly shamefaced.*) That's a lousy thing to say. I don't mean that.

TYRONE (*decides to ignore this*). He's been doing well on the paper. I was hoping he'd found the work he wants to do at last.

JAMIE (*sneering jealously again*). A hick town rag! Whatever bull they hand you, they tell me he's a pretty bum reporter. If he weren't your son – (*Ashamed again.*) No, that's not true! They're glad to have him, but it's the special stuff that gets him by. Some of the poems and parodies he's written are damned good. (*Grudgingly again.*) Not that they'd ever get him anywhere on the big time. (*Hastily.*) But he's certainly made a damned good start.

TYRONE. Yes. He's made a start. You used to talk about wanting to become a newspaper man but you were never willing to start at the bottom. You expected –

JAMIE. Oh, for Christ's sake, Papa! Can't you lay off me!

TYRONE (*stares at him – then looks away – after a pause*). It's damnable luck Edmund should be sick right now. It couldn't have come at a worse time for him. (*He adds, unable to conceal an almost furtive uneasiness.*) Or for your mother. It's damnable she should have this to upset her, just when she needs peace and freedom from worry. She's been so well in the two months since she came home. (*His voice grows husky and trembles a little.*) It's been heaven to me. This home has been a home again. But I needn't tell you, Jamie.

His son looks at him, for the first time with an understanding sympathy. It is as if suddenly a deep bond of common feeling existed between them in which their antagonisms could be forgotten.

JAMIE (*almost gently*). I've felt the same way, Papa.

TYRONE. Yes, this time you can see how strong and sure of herself she is. She's a different woman entirely from the other times. She has control of her nerves – or she had until Edmund got sick. Now you can feel her growing tense and frightened underneath. I wish to God we could keep the truth from her, but we can't if he has to be sent to a sanatorium. What makes it worse is her father died of consumption. She worshipped him and she's never forgotten. Yes, it will be hard for her. But she can do it! She has the will-power now! We must help her, Jamie, in every way we can!

JAMIE (*moved*). Of course, Papa. (*Hesitantly.*) Outside of nerves, she seems perfectly all right this morning.

TYRONE (*with hearty confidence now*). Never better. She's full of fun and mischief. (*Suddenly he frowns at* JAMIE *suspiciously.*) Why do you say, seems? Why shouldn't she be all right? What the hell do you mean?

JAMIE. Don't start jumping down my throat! God, Papa, this ought to be one thing we can talk over frankly without a battle.

TYRONE. I'm sorry, Jamie. (*Tensely.*) But go on and tell me –

JAMIE. There's nothing to tell. I was all wrong. It's just that last night – Well, you know how it is, I can't forget the past. I can't help being suspicious. Any more than you can. (*Bitterly.*) That's the hell of it. And it makes it hell for Mama! She watches us watching her –

TYRONE (*sadly*). I know. (*Tensely.*) Well, what was it? Can't you speak out?

JAMIE. Nothing, I tell you. Just my damned foolishness. Around three o'clock this morning, I woke up and heard her moving around in the spare room. Then she went to the bathroom. I pretended to be asleep. She stopped in the hall to listen, as if she wanted to make sure I was.

TYRONE (*with forced scorn*). For God's sake, is that all? She told me herself the foghorn kept her awake all night, and every night since Edmund's been sick she's been up and down, going to his room to see how he was.

JAMIE (*eagerly*). Yes, that's right, she did stop to listen outside his room. (*Hesitantly again.*) It was her being in the spare room that scared me. I couldn't help remembering that when she starts sleeping alone in there, it has always been a sign –

TYRONE. It isn't this time! It's easily explained. Where else could she go last night to get away from my snoring? (*He gives way to a burst of resentful anger.*) By God, how you live with a mind that sees nothing but the worst motives behind everything is beyond me!

JAMIE (*stung*). Don't pull that! I've just said I was all wrong. Don't you suppose I'm as glad of that as you are!

TYRONE (*mollifyingly*). I'm sure you are, Jamie. (*A pause. His expression becomes sombre. He speaks slowly with a superstitious dread.*) It would be like a curse she can't escape if worry over Edmund – It was in her long sickness after bringing him into the world that she first –

JAMIE. She didn't have anything to do with it!

TYRONE. I'm not blaming her.

JAMIE (*bitingly*). Then who are you blaming? Edmund, for being born?

TYRONE. You damned fool! No one was to blame.

JAMIE. The bastard of a doctor was! From what Mama's said, he was another cheap quack like Hardy! You wouldn't pay for a first-rate –

TYRONE. That's a lie! (*Furiously.*) So I'm to blame! That's what you're driving at, is it? You evil-minded loafer!

JAMIE (*warningly as he hears his mother in the dining-room*). Ssh!

TYRONE *gets hastily to his feet and goes to look out of the windows at right.* JAMIE *speaks with a complete change of tone.*

Well, if we're going to cut the front hedge today, we'd better go to work.

MARY *comes in from the back parlour. She gives a quick, suspicious glance from one to the other, her manner nervously self-conscious.*

TYRONE (*turns from the window – with an actor's heartiness*). Yes, it's too fine a morning to waste indoors arguing. Take a look out of the window, Mary. There's no fog in the harbour. I'm sure the spell of it we've had is over now.

MARY (*going to him*). I hope so, dear. (*To* JAMIE *forcing a smile.*) Did I actually hear you suggesting work on the front hedge, Jamie? Wonders will never cease! You must want pocket money badly.

JAMIE (*kiddingly*). When don't I? (*He winks at her, with a derisive glance at his father.*) I expect a salary of at least one large iron man at the end of the week – to carouse on!

MARY (*does not respond to his humour – her hands fluttering over the front of her dress*). What were you two arguing about?

JAMIE (*shrugs his shoulders*). The same old stuff.

MARY. I heard you say something about a doctor, and your father accusing you of being evil-minded.

JAMIE (*quickly*). Oh, that. I was saying again Doc Hardy isn't my idea of the world's greatest physician.

MARY (*knows he is lying – vaguely*). Oh. No, I wouldn't say he was, either. (*Changing the subject – forcing a smile.*) That Bridget! I thought I'd never get away. She told me all about her second cousin on the police force in St. Louis. (*Then with nervous irritation.*) Well, if you're going to work on the hedge why don't you go? (*Hastily.*) I mean, take advantage of the sunshine before the fog comes back. (*Strangely, as if talking aloud to herself.*) Because I know it will. (*Suddenly she is self-consciously aware that they are both staring fixedly at her – flurriedly, raising her hands.*) Or I should say, the rheumatism in my hands knows. It's a better weather prophet than you are, James. (*She stares at her hands with fascinated repulsion.*) Ugh! How ugly they are! Who'd ever believe they were once beautiful?

They stare at her with a growing dread.

TYRONE (*takes her hands and gently pushes them down*). Now, now, Mary. None of that foolishness. They're the sweetest hands in the world.

She smiles, her face lighting up, and kisses him gratefully. He turns to his son.

Come on, Jamie. Your mother's right to scold us. The way to start work is to start work. The hot sun will sweat some of that booze fat off your middle.

He opens the screen door and goes out on the porch and disappears down a flight of steps leading to the ground. JAMIE rises from his chair and, taking off his coat, goes to the door. At the door he turns back but avoids looking at her, and she does not look at him.

JAMIE (*with an awkward, uneasy tenderness*). We're all so proud of you, Mama, so darned happy.

She stiffens and stares at him with a frightened defiance. He flounders on.

But you've still got to be careful. You mustn't worry so much about Edmund. He'll be all right.

MARY (*with a stubborn, bitterly resentful look*). Of course, he'll be all right. And I don't know what you mean, warning me to be careful.

JAMIE (*rebuffed and hurt, shrugs his shoulders*). All right, Mama. I'm sorry I spoke.

He goes out on the porch. She waits rigidly until he disappears down the steps. Then she sinks down in the chair he had occupied, her face betraying a frightened, furtive desperation, her hands roving over the table top, aimlessly moving objects around. She hears EDMUND descending the stairs in the front hall. As he nears the bottom he has a fit of coughing. She springs to her feet, as if she wanted to run away from the sound, and goes quickly to the windows at right. She is looking out, apparently calm, as he enters from the front parlour, a book in one hand. She turns to him, her lips set in a welcoming, motherly smile.

MARY. Here you are. I was just going upstairs to look for you.

EDMUND. I waited until they went out. I don't want to mix up in any arguments. I feel too rotten.

MARY (*almost resentfully*). Oh, I'm sure you don't feel half as badly as you make out. You're such a baby. You like to get us worried so we'll make a fuss over you. (*Hastily.*) I'm only teasing, dear. I know how miserably uncomfortable you must be. But you feel better today, don't you? (*Worriedly, taking his arm*). All the same, you've grown much too thin. You need to rest all you can. Sit down and I'll make you comfortable.

He sits down in the rocking-chair and she puts a pillow behind his back.

There. How's that?

EDMUND. Grand. Thanks, Mama.

MARY (*kisses him – tenderly*). All you need is your mother to nurse you. Big as you are, you're still the baby of the family to me, you know.

EDMUND (*takes her hand – with deep seriousness*). Never mind me. You take care of yourself. That's all that counts.

MARY (*evading his eyes*). But I am, dear. (*Forcing a laugh.*) Heavens, don't you see how fat I've grown! I'll have to have all my dresses let out. (*She turns away and goes to the windows at right. She attempts a light, amused tone.*) They've started clipping the hedge. Poor Jamie! How he hates working in front where everyone passing can see him. There go the Chatfields in their new Mercedes. It's a beautiful car, isn't it? Not like our secondhand Packard. Poor Jamie! He bent almost under the hedge so they wouldn't notice him. They bowed to your father and he bowed back as if he were taking a curtain call. In that filthy old suit I've tried to make him throw away. (*Her voice has grown bitter.*) Really, he ought to have more pride than to make such a show of himself.

EDMUND. He's right not to give a damn what anyone thinks. Jamie's a fool to care about the Chatfields. For Pete's sake, who ever heard of them outside this hick burg?

MARY (*with satisfaction*). No one. You're quite right, Edmund. Big frogs in a small puddle. It is stupid of Jamie. (*She pauses, looking out of the window – then with an undercurrent of lonely yearning.*) Still, the Chatfields and people like them stand for something. I mean they have decent, presentable homes they don't have to be ashamed of. They have friends who entertain them and whom they entertain. They're not cut off from everyone. (*She turns back from the window.*) Not that I want anything to do with them. I've always hated this town and everyone in it. You know that. I never wanted to live here in the first place, but your father liked it and insisted on building this house, and I've had to come here every summer.

EDMUND. Well, it's better than spending the summer in a New York hotel, isn't it? And this town's not so bad. I like it well enough. I suppose because it's the only home we've had.

MARY. I've never felt it was my home. It was wrong from the start. Everything was done in the cheapest way. Your father would never spend the money to make it right. It's just as well we haven't any friends here. I'd be ashamed to have them step in the door. But he's never wanted family friends. He hates calling on people, or receiving them. All he likes is to hobnob with men at the Club or in a bar-room. Jamie and you are the same way, but you're not to blame. You've never had a chance to meet decent people here. I know you both would have been so different if you'd been able to associate with nice girls instead of – You'd never have disgraced yourselves as you have, so that now no respectable parents will let their daughters be seen with you.

EDMUND (*irritably*). Oh, Mama, forget it! Who cares? Jamie and I would be bored stiff. And about the Old Man, what's the use of talking? You can't change him.

MARY (*mechanically rebuking*). Don't call your father the Old Man. You should have more respect. (*Then dully.*) I know it's useless to talk. But sometimes I feel so lonely. (*Her lips quiver and she keeps her head turned away.*)

EDMUND. Anyway, you've got to be fair, Mama. It may have been all his fault in the beginning, but you know that later on, even if he'd wanted to, we couldn't have had people here – (*He flounders guiltily.*) I mean, you wouldn't have wanted them.

MARY (*wincing – her lips quivering pitifully*). Don't. I can't bear having you remind me.

EDMUND. Don't take it that way! Please, Mama! I'm trying to help. Because it's bad for you to forget. The right way is to remember. So you'll always be on your guard. You know what's happened before. (*Miserably.*) God, Mama, you know I hate to remind you. I'm doing it because it's been so wonderful having you home the way you've been, and it would be terrible –

MARY (*strickenly*). Please, dear. I know you mean it for the best, but – (*A defensive uneasiness comes into her voice again.*) I don't understand why you should suddenly say such things. What put it in your mind this morning?

EDMUND (*evasively*): Nothing. Just because I feel rotten and blue, I suppose.

MARY. Tell me the truth. Why are you so suspicious all of a sudden?

EDMUND. I'm not!

MARY. Oh, yes you are. I can feel it. Your father and Jamie, too – particularly Jamie.

EDMUND. Now don't start imagining things, Mama.

MARY (*her hands fluttering*). It makes it so much harder, living in this atmosphere of constant suspicion, knowing everyone is spying on me, and none of you believe in me, or trust me.

EDMUND. That's crazy, Mama. We do trust you.

MARY. If there was only some place I could go to get away for a day, or even an afternoon, some woman friend I could talk to – not about anything serious, simply laugh and gossip and forget for a while – someone besides the servants – that stupid Cathleen!

EDMUND (*gets up worriedly and puts his arm around her*). Stop it, Mama. You're getting yourself worked up over nothing.

MARY. Your father goes out. He meets his friends in bar-rooms or at the Club. You and Jamie have the boys you know. You go out. But I am alone. I've always been alone.

EDMUND (*soothingly*). Come now! You know that's a fib. One of us always stays around to keep you company, or goes with you in the automobile when you take a drive.

MARY (*bitterly*). Because you're afraid to trust me alone! (*She turns on him – sharply.*) I insist you tell me why you act so differently this morning – why you felt you had to remind me –

EDMUND (*hesitates – then blurts out guiltily*). It's stupid. It's just that I wasn't asleep when you came in my room last night. You didn't go back to your and Papa's room. You went in the spare room for the rest of the night.

MARY. Because your father's snoring was driving me crazy! For heaven's sake, haven't I often used the spare room as my bedroom? (*Bitterly.*) But I see what you thought. That was when –

EDMUND (*too vehemently*). I didn't think anything!

MARY. So you pretended to be asleep in order to spy on me!

EDMUND. No! I did it because I knew if you found out I was feverish and couldn't sleep, it would upset you.

MARY. Jamie was pretending to be asleep, too, I'm sure, and I suppose your father –

EDMUND. Stop it, Mama!

MARY. Oh, I can't bear it, Edmund, when even you – ! (*Her hands flutter up to pat her hair in their aimless, distracted way. Suddenly a strange undercurrent of revengefulness comes into her voice.*) It would serve all of you right if it was true!

EDMUND. Mama! Don't say that! That's the way you talk when –

MARY. Stop suspecting me! Please, dear! You hurt me! I couldn't sleep because I was thinking about you. That's the real reason! I've been so worried ever since you've been sick. (*She puts her arms around him and hugs him with a frightened, protective tenderness.*)

EDMUND (*soothingly*). That's foolishness. You know it's only a bad cold.

MARY. Yes, of course, I know that!

EDMUND. But listen, Mama. I want you to promise me that even if it should turn out to be something worse, you'll know I'll soon be all right again, anyway, and you won't worry yourself sick, and you'll keep on taking care of yourself –

MARY (*frightenedly*). I won't listen when you're so silly! There's absolutely no reason to talk as if you expected something dreadful! Of course, I promise you. I give you my sacred word of honour! (*Then with a sad bitterness.*) But I suppose you're remembering I've promised before on my word of honour.

EDMUND. No!

MARY (*her bitterness receding into a resigned helplessness*). I'm not blaming you, dear. How can you help it? How can any one of us forget? (*Strangely.*) That's what makes it so hard – for all of us. We can't forget.

EDMUND (*grabs her shoulder*). Mama! Stop it!

MARY (*forcing a smile*). All right, dear. I didn't mean to be so gloomy. Don't mind me. Here. Let me feel your head. Why, it's nice and cool. You certainly haven't any fever now.

EDMUND. Forget! It's you –

MARY. But I'm quite all right, dear. (*With a quick, strange, calculating, almost sly glance at him.*) Except I naturally feel tired and nervous this morning, after such a bad night. I really ought to go upstairs and lie down until lunch-time and take a nap. (*He gives her an instinctive look of suspicion – then, ashamed of himself, looks quickly away. She hurries on nervously.*) What are you going to do? Read here? It would be much better for you to go out in the fresh air and sunshine. But don't get overheated, remember. Be sure and wear a hat. (*She stops, looking straight at him now. He avoids her eyes. There is a tense pause. Then she speaks jeeringly.*) Or are you afraid to trust me alone?

EDMUND (*tormentedly*). No! Can't you stop talking like that? I think you ought to take a nap. (*He goes to the screen door – forcing a joking tone.*) I'll go down and help Jamie bear up. I love to lie in the shade and watch him work.

He forces a laugh in which she makes herself join. Then he goes out on the porch and disappears down the steps. Her first reaction is one of relief. She appears to relax. She sinks down in one of the wicker armchairs at rear of table and leans her head back, closing her eyes. But suddenly she grows terribly tense again. Her eyes open and she strains forward, seized by a fit of nervous panic. She begins a desperate battle with herself. Her long fingers, warped and knotted by rheumatism, drum on the arms of the chair, driven by an insistent life of their own, without her consent.

ACT TWO

Scene One

Scene. The same. It is around quarter to one. No sunlight comes into the room now through the windows at right. Outside the day is still fine but increasingly sultry, with a faint haziness in the air which softens the glare of the sun.

EDMUND sits in the armchair at left of table, reading a book. Or rather he is trying to concentrate on it but cannot. He seems to be listening for some sound from upstairs. His manner is nervously apprehensive and he looks more sickly than in the previous act.

The second girl, CATHLEEN, enters from the back parlour. She carries a tray on which is a bottle of bonded Bourbon, several whiskey glasses, and a pitcher of ice water. She is a buxom Irish peasant, in her early twenties, with a red-cheeked comely face, black hair and blue eyes – amiable, ignorant, clumsy, and possessed by a dense, well-meaning stupidity. She puts the tray on the table. EDMUND pretends to be so absorbed in his book he does not notice her, but she ignores this.

CATHLEEN (*with garrulous familiarity*). Here's the whiskey. It'll be lunch-time soon. Will I call your father and Mister Jamie, or will you?

EDMUND (*without looking up from his book*). You do it.

CATHLEEN. It's a wonder your father wouldn't look at his watch once in a while. He's a divil for making the meals late, and then Bridget curses me as if I was to blame. But he's a grand handsome man, if he is old. You'll never see the day you're as good-looking – nor Mister Jamie, either. (*She chuckles.*) I'll wager Mister Jamie wouldn't miss the time to stop work and have his drop of whiskey if he had a watch to his name!

EDMUND (*gives up trying to ignore her and grins*). You win that one.

CATHLEEN. And here's another I'd win, that you're making me call them so you can sneak a drink before they come.

EDMUND. Well, I hadn't thought of that –

CATHLEEN. Oh no, not you! Butter wouldn't melt in your mouth, I suppose.

EDMUND. But now you suggest it –

CATHLEEN (*suddenly primly virtuous*). I'd never suggest a man or a woman touch drink, Mister Edmund. Sure didn't it kill an uncle of mine in the old country. (*Relenting.*) Still, a drop now and then is no harm when you're in low spirits, or have a bad cold.

EDMUND. Thanks for handing me a good excuse. (*Then with forced casualness.*) You'd better call my mother, too.

CATHLEEN. What for? She's always on time without any calling. God bless her, she has some consideration for the help.

EDMUND. She's been taking a nap.

CATHLEEN. She wasn't asleep when I finished my work upstairs a while back. She was lying down in the spare room with her eyes wide open. She'd a terrible headache, she said.

EDMUND (*his casualness more forced*). Oh well then, just call my father.

CATHLEEN (*goes to the screen door, grumbling good-naturedly*). No wonder my feet kill me each night. I won't walk out in this heat and get sunstroke. I'll call from the porch.

She goes out on the side porch, letting the screen door slam behind her, and disappears on her way to the front porch. A moment later she is heard shouting.

Mister Tyrone! Mister Jamie! It's time!

EDMUND, *who has been staring frightenedly before him, forgetting his book, springs to his feet nervously.*

EDMUND. God, what a wench!

He grabs the bottle and pours a drink, adds ice water and drinks. As he does so, he hears someone coming in the front door. He puts the glass hastily on the tray and sits down again, opening his book. JAMIE comes in from the front parlour, his coat over his arm. He has taken off collar and tie and carries them in his hand. He is wiping sweat from his forehead with a handkerchief. EDMUND looks up as if his reading was interrupted. JAMIE takes one look at the bottle and glasses and smiles cynically.

JAMIE. Sneaking one, eh? Cut out the bluff, Kid. You're a rottener actor than I am.

EDMUND (*grins*). Yes, I grabbed one while the going was good.

JAMIE (*puts a hand affectionately on his shoulder*). That's better. Why kid me? We're pals, aren't we?

EDMUND. I wasn't sure it was you coming.

JAMIE. I made the Old Man look at his watch. I was halfway up the walk when Cathleen burst into song. Our wild Irish lark! She ought to be a train announcer.

EDMUND. That's what drove me to drink. Why don't you sneak one while you've got a chance?

JAMIE. I was thinking of that little thing. (*He goes quickly to the window at right.*) The Old Man was talking to old Captain Turner. Yes, he's still at it. (*He comes back and takes a drink.*) And now to cover up from his eagle eye. (*He memorizes the level in the bottle after every drink. He measures two drinks of water and pours them in the whiskey bottle and shakes it up.*) There. That fixes it. (*He pours water in the glass and sets it on the table by* EDMUND.) And here's the water you've been drinking.

EDMUND. Fine! You don't think it will fool him, do you?

JAMIE. Maybe not, but he can't prove it. (*Putting on his collar and tie.*) I hope he doesn't forget lunch listening to himself talk. I'm hungry. (*He sits across the table from* EDMUND – *irritably.*) That's what I hate about working down in front. He puts on an act for every damned fool that comes along.

EDMUND (*gloomily*). You're in luck to be hungry. The way I feel I don't care if I ever eat again.

JAMIE (*gives him a glance of concern*). Listen, Kid. You know me. I've never lectured you, but Doctor Hardy was right when he told you to cut out the redeye.

EDMUND. Oh, I'm going to after he hands me the bad news this afternoon. A few before then won't make any difference.

JAMIE (*hesitates – then slowly*). I'm glad you've got your mind prepared for bad news. It won't be such a jolt. (*He catches* EDMUND *staring at him.*) I mean, it's a cinch you're really sick, and it would be wrong dope to kid yourself.

EDMUND (*disturbed*). I'm not. I know how rotten I feel, and the fever and chills I get at night are no joke. I think Doctor Hardy's last guess was right. It must be the damned malaria come back on me.

JAMIE. Maybe, but don't be too sure.

EDMUND. Why? What do you think it is?

JAMIE. Hell, how would I know? I'm no Doc. (*Abruptly.*) Where's Mama?

EDMUND. Upstairs.

JAMIE (*looks at him sharply*). When did she go up?

EDMUND. Oh, about the time I came down to the hedge, I guess. She said she was going to take a nap.

JAMIE. You didn't tell me –

EDMUND (*defensively*). Why should I? What about it? She was tired out. She didn't get much sleep last night.

JAMIE. I know she didn't.

A pause. The brothers avoid looking at each other.

EDMUND. That damned foghorn kept me awake, too.

Another pause.

JAMIE. She's been upstairs alone all morning, eh? You haven't seen her?

EDMUND. No. I've been reading here. I wanted to give her a chance to sleep.

JAMIE. Is she coming down to lunch?

EDMUND. Of course.

JAMIE (*dryly*). No of course about it. She might not want any lunch. Or she might start having most of her meals alone upstairs. That's happened, hasn't it?

EDMUND (*with frightened resentment*). Cut it out, Jamie! Can't you think anything but – ? (*Persuasively.*) You're all wrong to suspect anything. Cathleen saw her not long ago. Mama didn't tell her she wouldn't be down to lunch.

JAMIE. Then she wasn't taking a nap?

EDMUND. Not right then, but she was lying down, Cathleen said.

JAMIE. In the spare room?

EDMUND. Yes. For Pete's sake, what of it?

JAMIE (*bursts out*). You damned fool! Why did you leave her alone so long? Why didn't you stick around?

EDMUND. Because she accused me – and you and Papa – of spying on her all the time and not trusting her. She made me feel ashamed. I know how rotten it must be for her. And she promised on her sacred word of honour –

JAMIE (*with a bitter weariness*). You ought to know that doesn't mean anything.

EDMUND. It does this time!

JAMIE. That's what we thought the other times. (*He leans over the table to give his brother's arm an affectionate grasp.*) Listen, Kid, I know you think I'm a cynical bastard, but remember I've seen a lot more of this game than you have. You never knew what was really wrong until you were in prep school. Papa and I kept it from you. But I was wise ten years or more before we had to tell you. I know the game backwards and I've been thinking all morning of the way she acted last night when she thought we were asleep. I haven't been able to think of anything else. And now you tell me she got you to leave her alone upstairs all morning.

EDMUND. She didn't! You're crazy!

JAMIE (*placatingly*). All right, Kid. Don't start a battle with me. I hope as much as you do I'm crazy. I've been as happy as hell because I'd really begun to believe that this time – (*He stops – looking through the front parlour toward the hall – lowering his voice, hurriedly.*) She's coming downstairs. You win on that. I guess I'm a damned suspicious louse.

They grow tense with a hopeful, fearful expectancy. JAMIE mutters.

Damn! I wish I'd grabbed another drink.

EDMUND. Me, too.

He coughs nervously and this brings on a real fit of coughing. JAMIE glances at him with worried pity. MARY enters from the front parlour. At first one notices no change except that she appears to be less nervous, to be more as she was when we first saw her after breakfast, but then one becomes aware that her eyes are brighter, and there is a peculiar detachment in her voice and manner, as if she were a little withdrawn from her words and actions.

MARY (*goes worriedly to EDMUND and puts her arm around him*). You mustn't cough like that. It's bad for your throat. You don't want to get a sore throat on top of your cold.

She kisses him. He stops coughing and gives her a quick apprehensive glance, but if his suspicions are aroused her tenderness makes him renounce them and he believes what he wants to believe for the moment. On the other hand, JAMIE *knows after one probing look at her that his suspicions are justified. His eyes fall to stare at the floor, his face sets in an expression of embittered, defensive cynicism.* MARY *goes on, half sitting on the arm of* EDMUND'*s chair, her arm around him, so her face is above and behind his and he cannot look into her eyes.*

But I seem to be always picking on you, telling you don't do this and don't do that. Forgive me, dear. It's just that I want to take care of you.

EDMUND. I know, Mama. How about you? Do you feel rested?

MARY. Yes, ever so much better. I've been lying down ever since you went out. It's what I needed after such a restless night. I don't feel nervous now.

EDMUND. That's fine.

He pats her hand on his shoulder. JAMIE *gives him a strange, almost contemptuous glance, wondering if his brother can really mean this.* EDMUND *does not notice but his mother does.*

MARY (*in a forced teasing tone*). Good heavens, how down in the mouth you look, Jamie! What's the matter now?

JAMIE (*without looking at her*). Nothing.

MARY. Oh, I'd forgotten you've been working on the front hedge. That accounts for your sinking into the dumps, doesn't it?

JAMIE. If you want to think so, Mama.

MARY (*keeping her tone*). Well, that's the effect it always has, isn't it? What a big baby you are! Isn't he, Edmund?

EDMUND. He's certainly a fool to care what anyone thinks.

MARY (*strangely*). Yes, the only way is to make yourself not care. (*She catches* JAMIE *giving her a bitter glance and changes the subject.*) Where is your father? I heard Cathleen call him.

EDMUND. Gabbing with old Captain Turner, Jamie says. He'll be late, as usual.

JAMIE *gets up and goes to the windows at right, glad of an excuse to turn his back.*

MARY. I've told Cathleen time and again she must go wherever he is and tell him. The idea of screaming as if this were a cheap boardinghouse!

JAMIE (*looking out of the window*). She's down there now. (*Sneeringly.*) Interrupting the famous Beautiful Voice! She should have more respect.

MARY (*sharply – letting her resentment toward him come out*). It's you who should have more respect! Stop sneering at your father! I won't have it! You ought to be proud you're his son! He may have his faults. Who hasn't? But he's worked hard all his life. He made his way up from ignorance and poverty to the top of his profession! Everyone else admires him and you should be the last one to sneer – you, who, thanks to him, have never had to work hard in your life!

Stung, JAMIE has turned to stare at her with accusing antagonism. Her eyes waver guiltily and she adds in a tone which begins to placate.

Remember your father is getting old, Jamie. You really ought to show more consideration.

JAMIE. *I* ought to?

EDMUND (*uneasily*). Oh, dry up, Jamie!

JAMIE looks out of the window again.

And, for Pete's sake, Mama, why jump on Jamie all of a sudden?

MARY (*bitterly*). Because he's always sneering at someone else, looking for the worst weakness in everyone. (*Then with a strange, abrupt change to a detached, impersonal tone.*) But I suppose life has made him like that, and he can't help it. None of us can help the things life has done to us. They're done before you realize it, and once they're done they make you do other things until at last everything comes between you and what you'd like to be, and you've lost your true self for ever.

EDMUND is made apprehensive by her strangeness. He tries to look up in her eyes but she keeps them averted. JAMIE turns to her – then looks quickly out of the window again.

JAMIE (*dully*). I'm hungry. I wish the Old Man would get a move on. It's a rotten trick the way he keeps meals waiting, and then beefs because they're spoiled.

MARY (*with a resentment that has a quality of being automatic and on the surface while inwardly she is indifferent*). Yes, it's very trying,

Jamie. You don't know how trying. You don't have to keep house with summer servants who don't care because they know it isn't a permanent position. The really good servants are all with people who have homes and not merely summer places. And your father won't even pay the wages the best summer help ask. So every year I have stupid, lazy greenhorns to deal with. But you've heard me say this a thousand times. So has he, but it goes in one ear and out the other. He thinks money spent on a home is money wasted. He's lived too much in hotels. Never the best hotels, of course. Second-rate hotels. He doesn't understand a home. He doesn't feel at home in it. And yet, he wants a home. He's even proud of having this shabby place. He loves it here. (*She laughs – a hopeless and yet amused laugh.*) It's really funny, when you come to think of it. He's a peculiar man.

EDMUND (*again attempting uneasily to look up in her eyes*). What makes you ramble on like that, Mama?

MARY (*quickly casual – patting his cheek*). Why, nothing in particular, dear. It *is* foolish.

As she speaks, CATHLEEN *enters from the back parlour.*

CATHLEEN (*volubly*). Lunch is ready, Ma'am. I went down to Mister Tyrone, like you ordered, and he said he'd come right away, but he kept on talking to that man, telling him of the time when –

MARY (*indifferently*). All right, Cathleen. Tell Bridget I'm sorry but she'll have to wait a few minutes until Mister Tyrone is here.

CATHLEEN *mutters, 'Yes, Ma'am', and goes off through the back parlour, grumbling to herself.*

JAMIE. Damn it! Why don't you go ahead without him? He's told us to.

MARY (*with a remote, amused smile*). He doesn't mean it. Don't you know your father yet? He'd be so terribly hurt.

EDMUND (*jumps up – as if he was glad of an excuse to leave*). I'll make him get a move on. (*He goes out on the side porch. A moment later he is heard calling from the porch exasperatedly.*) Hey! Papa! Come on! We can't wait all day!

MARY *has risen from the arm of the chair. Her hands play restlessly over the table top. She does not look at* JAMIE *but she feels the cynically appraising glance he gives her face and hands.*

MARY (*tensely*). Why do you stare like that?

JAMIE. You know. (*He turns back to the window.*)

MARY. I don't know.

JAMIE. Oh, for God's sake, do you think you can fool me, Mama? I'm not blind.

MARY (*looks directly at him now, her face set again in an expression of blank, stubborn denial*). I don't know what you're talking about.

JAMIE. No? Take a look at your eyes in the mirror!

EDMUND (*coming in from the porch*). I got Papa moving. He'll be here in a minute. (*With a glance from one to the other, which his mother avoids – uneasily.*) What's happened? What's the matter, Mama?

MARY (*disturbed by his coming, gives way to a flurry of guilty, nervous excitement*). Your brother ought to be ashamed of himself. He's been insinuating I don't know what.

EDMUND (*turns on* JAMIE). God damn you!

He takes a threatening step toward him. JAMIE *turns his back with a shrug and looks out of the window.*

MARY (*more upset, grabs* EDMUND's *arm – excitedly*). Stop this at once, do you hear me? How dare you use such language before me! (*Abruptly her tone and manner change to the strange detachment she has shown before.*) It's wrong to blame your brother. He can't help being what the past has made him. Any more than your father can. Or you. Or I.

EDMUND (*frightenedly – with a desperate hoping against hope*). He's a liar! It's a lie, isn't it, Mama?

MARY (*keeping her eyes averted*). What is a lie? Now you're talking in riddles like Jamie. (*Then her eyes meet his stricken, accusing look. She stammers.*) Edmund! Don't! (*She looks away and her manner instantly regains the quality of strange detachment – calmly.*) There's your father coming up the steps now. I must tell Bridget.

She goes through the back parlour. EDMUND *moves slowly to his chair. He looks sick and hopeless.*

JAMIE (*from the window, without looking around*). Well?

EDMUND (*refusing to admit anything to his brother yet – weakly defiant*). Well, what? You're a liar.

JAMIE *again shrugs his shoulders. The screen door on the front porch is heard closing.* EDMUND *says dully.*

Here's Papa. I hope he loosens up with the old bottle.

TYRONE *comes in through the front parlour. He is putting on his coat.*

TYRONE. Sorry I'm late. Captain Turner stopped to talk and once he starts gabbing you can't get away from him.

JAMIE (*without turning – drily*). You mean once he starts listening.

His father regards him with dislike. He comes to the table with a quick measuring look at the bottle of whiskey. Without turning, JAMIE *senses this.*

It's all right. The level in the bottle hasn't changed.

TYRONE. I wasn't noticing that. (*He adds caustically.*) As if it proved anything with you around. I'm on to your tricks.

EDMUND (*dully*). Did I hear you say, let's all have a drink?

TYRONE (*frowns at him*). Jamie is welcome after his hard morning's work, but I won't invite you. Doctor Hardy –

EDMUND. To hell with Doctor Hardy! One isn't going to kill me. I feel – all in, Papa.

TYRONE (*with a worried look at him – putting on a false heartiness*). Come along, then. It's before a meal and I've always found that good whiskey, taken in moderation as an appetizer, is the best of tonics.

EDMUND *gets up as his father passes the bottle to him. He pours a big drink.* TYRONE *frowns admonishingly.*

I said, in moderation. (*He pours his own drink and passes the bottle to* JAMIE, *grumbling.*) It'd be a waste of breath mentioning moderation to you.

Ignoring the hint, JAMIE *pours a big drink. His father scowls – then, giving it up, resumes his hearty air, raising his glass.*

Well, here's health and happiness!

EDMUND *gives a bitter laugh.*

EDMUND. That's a joke!

TYRONE. What is?

EDMUND. Nothing. Here's how.

They drink.

TYRONE (*becomes aware of the atmosphere*). What's the matter here? There's gloom in the air you could cut with a knife. (*Turns on* JAMIE *resentfully*.) You got the drink you were after, didn't you? Why are you wearing that gloomy look on your mug?

JAMIE (*shrugging his shoulders*). You won't be singing a song yourself soon.

EDMUND. Shut up, Jamie.

TYRONE (*uneasy now – changing the subject*). I thought lunch was ready. I'm hungry as a hunter. Where is your mother?

MARY (*returning through the back parlour, calls*). Here I am. (*She comes in. She is excited and self-conscious. As she talks, she glances everywhere except at any of their faces.*) I've had to calm down Bridget. She's in a tantrum over your being late again, and I don't blame her. If your lunch is dried up from waiting in the oven, she said it served you right, you could like it or leave it for all she cared. (*With increasing excitement.*) Oh, I'm so sick and tired of pretending this is a home! You won't help me! You won't put yourself out the least bit! You don't know how to act in a home! You don't really want one! You never have wanted one – never since the day we were married! You should have remained a bachelor and lived in second-rate hotels and entertained your friends in bar-rooms! (*She adds strangely, as if she were now talking aloud to herself rather than to* TYRONE.) Then nothing would ever have happened.

They stare at her. TYRONE *knows now. He suddenly looks a tired, bitterly sad old man.* EDMUND *glances at his father and sees that he knows, but he still cannot help trying to warn his mother.*

EDMUND. Mama! Stop talking. Why don't we go in to lunch.

MARY (*starts and at once the quality of unnatural detachment settles on her face again. She even smiles with an ironical amusement to herself*). Yes, it is inconsiderate of me to dig up the past, when I know your father and Jamie must be hungry. (*Putting her arm around* EDMUND*'s shoulder – with a fond solicitude which is at the same time remote.*) I do hope you have an appetite, dear. You really must eat more. (*Her eyes become fixed on the whiskey glass on the table beside him – sharply.*) Why is that glass there? Did you take a drink? Oh, how can you be such a fool? Don't you know it's the worst thing? (*She turns on* TYRONE.) You're to blame, James.

How could you let him? Do you want to kill him? Don't you remember my father? He wouldn't stop after he was stricken. He said doctors were fools! He thought, like you, that whiskey is a good tonic! (*A look of terror comes into her eyes and she stammers.*) But, of course, there's no comparison at all. I don't know why I – Forgive me for scolding you, James. One small drink won't hurt Edmund. It might be good for him, if it gives him an appetite.

She pats EDMUND's *cheek playfully, the strange detachment again in her manner. He jerks his head away. She seems not to notice, but she moves instinctively away.*

JAMIE (*roughly, to hide his tense nerves*). For God's sake, let's eat. I've been working in the damned dirt under the hedge all morning. I've earned my grub. (*He comes around behind his father, not looking at his mother, and grabs* EDMUND's *shoulder.*) Come on, Kid. Let's put on the feed bag.

EDMUND *gets up, keeping his eyes averted from his mother. They pass her, heading for the back parlour.*

TYRONE (*dully*). Yes, you go in with your mother, lads. I'll join you in a second.

But they keep on without waiting for her. She looks at their backs with a helpless hurt and, as they enter the back parlour, starts to follow them. TYRONE's *eyes are on her, sad and condemning. She feels them and turns sharply without meeting his stare.*

MARY. Why do you look at me like that? (*Her hands flutter up to pat her hair.*) Is it my hair coming down? I was so worn out from last night. I thought I'd better lie down this morning. I drowsed off and had a nice refreshing nap. But I'm sure I fixed my hair again when I woke up. (*Forcing a laugh.*) Although, as usual, I couldn't find my glasses. (*Sharply.*) Please stop staring! One would think you were accusing me – (*Then pleadingly.*) James! You don't understand!

TYRONE (*with dull anger*). I understand that I've been a God-damned fool to believe in you! (*He walks away from her to pour himself a big drink.*)

MARY (*her face again sets in stubborn defiance*). I don't know what you mean by 'believing in me'. All I've felt was distrust and spying and suspicion. (*Then accusingly.*) Why are you having another drink? You never have more than one before lunch. (*Bitterly.*) I know what to expect. You will be drunk tonight.

Well, it won't be the first time, will it – or the thousandth? (*Again she bursts out pleadingly.*) Oh, James, please! You don't understand! I'm so worried about Edmund! I'm so afraid he –

TYRONE. I don't want to listen to your excuses, Mary.

MARY (*strickenly*). Excuses? You mean – ? Oh, you can't believe that of me! You mustn't believe that, James! (*Then slipping away into her strange detachment – quite casually.*) Shall we not go in to lunch, dear? I don't want anything but I know you're hungry.

He walks slowly to where she stands in the doorway. He walks like an old man. As he reaches her she bursts out piteously.

James! I tried so hard! I tried so hard! Please believe – !

TYRONE (*moved in spite of himself – helplessly*). I suppose you did, Mary. (*Then grief-strickenly.*) For the love of God, why couldn't you have the strength to keep on?

MARY (*her face setting into that stubborn denial again*). I don't know what you're talking about. Have the strength to keep on what?

TYRONE (*hopelessly*). Never mind. It's no use now.

He moves on and she keeps beside him as they disappear in the back parlour.

ACT TWO

Scene Two

Scene. The same, about half an hour later. The tray with the bottle of whiskey has been removed from the table. The family are returning from lunch as the curtain rises. MARY is the first to enter from the back parlour. Her husband follows. He is not with her as he was in the similar entrance after breakfast at the opening of Act One. He avoids touching her or looking at her. There is condemnation in his face, mingled now with the beginning of an old weary, helpless resignation. JAMIE and EDMUND follow their father. JAMIE's face is hard with defensive cynicism. EDMUND tries to copy this defence but without success. He plainly shows he is heartsick as well as physically ill.

MARY is terribly nervous again, as if the strain of sitting through lunch with them had been too much for her. Yet at the same time, in contrast to this, her expression shows more of that strange aloofness which seems to stand apart from her nerves and the anxieties which harry them.

She is talking as she enters – a stream of words that issues casually, in a routine of family conversation, from her mouth. She appears indifferent to the fact that their thoughts are not on what she is saying any more than her own are. As she talks, she comes to the left of the table and stands, facing front, one hand fumbling with the bosom of her dress, the other playing over the table top. TYRONE lights a cigar and goes to the screen door, staring out. JAMIE fills a pipe from a jar on top of the bookcase at rear. He lights it as he goes to look out of the window at right. EDMUND sits in a chair by the table, turned half away from his mother so he does not have to watch her.

MARY. It's no use finding fault with Bridget. She doesn't listen. I can't threaten her, or she'd threaten she'd leave. And she does do her best at times. It's too bad they seem to be just the times you're sure to be late, James. Well, there's this consolation: it's difficult to tell from her cooking whether she's doing her best or her worst. (*She gives a little laugh of detached amusement – indifferently.*) Never mind. The summer will soon be over, thank goodness. Your season will open again and we can go back to second-rate hotels and trains. I hate them, too, but at least I don't expect them to be like a home, and there's no

housekeeping to worry about. It's unreasonable to expect
Bridget or Cathleen to act as if this was a home. They know it
isn't as well as we know it. It never has been and it never will
be.

TYRONE (*bitterly without turning around*). No, it never can be now.
But it was once, before you —

MARY (*her face instantly set in blank denial*). Before I what? (*There
is a dead silence. She goes on with a return of her detached air.*) No,
no. Whatever you mean, it isn't true, dear. It was never a
home. You've always preferred the Club or a bar-room. And
for me it's always been as lonely as a dirty room in a one-night
stand hotel. In a real home one is never lonely. You forget I
know from experience what a home is like. I gave up one to
marry you — my father's home. (*At once, through an association of
ideas she turns to* EDMUND. *Her manner becomes tenderly solicitous,
but there is the strange quality of detachment in it.*) I'm worried
about you, Edmund. You hardly touched a thing at lunch.
That's no way to take care of yourself. It's all right for me not
to have an appetite. I've been growing too fat. But you must
eat. (*Coaxingly maternal.*) Promise me you will, dear, for my
sake.

EDMUND (*dully*). Yes, Mama.

MARY (*pats his cheek as he tries not to shrink away*). That's a good
boy.

*There is another pause of dead silence. Then the telephone in the front
hall rings and all of them stiffen startledly.*

TYRONE (*hastily*). I'll answer. McGuire said he'd call me. (*He goes
out through the front parlour.*)

MARY (*indifferently*). McGuire. He must have another piece of
property on his list that no one would think of buying except
your father. It doesn't matter any more, but it's always seemed
to me your father could afford to keep on buying property but
never to give me a home. (*She stops to listen as* TYRONE's *voice is
heard from the hall.*)

TYRONE. Hello. (*With forced heartiness.*) Oh, how are you,
Doctor?

JAMIE *turns from the window.* MARY's *fingers play more rapidly on
the table top.* TYRONE's *voice, trying to conceal, reveals that he is
hearing bad news.*

I see – (*Hurriedly.*) Well, you'll explain all about it when you see him this afternoon. Yes, he'll be in without fail. Four o'clock. I'll drop in myself and have a talk with you before that. I have to go uptown on business, anyway. Goodbye, Doctor.

EDMUND (*dully*). That didn't sound like glad tidings.

JAMIE *gives him a pitying glance – then looks out of the window again.* MARY's *face is terrified and her hands flutter distractedly.* TYRONE *comes in. The strain is obvious in his casualness as he addresses* EDMUND.

TYRONE. It was Doctor Hardy. He wants you to be sure and see him at four.

EDMUND (*dully*). What did he say? Not that I give a damn now.

MARY (*bursts out excitedly*). I wouldn't believe him if he swore on a stack of Bibles. You mustn't pay attention to a word he says, Edmund.

TYRONE (*sharply*). Mary!

MARY (*more excitedly*). Oh, we all realize why you like him, James! Because he's cheap! But please don't try to tell me! I know all about Doctor Hardy. Heaven knows I ought to after all these years. He's an ignorant fool! There should be a law to keep men like him from practising. He hasn't the slightest idea – When you're in agony and half insane, he sits and holds your hand and delivers sermons on will-power! (*Her face is drawn in an expression of intense suffering by the memory. For the moment, she loses all caution. With bitter hatred.*) He deliberately humiliates you! He makes you beg and plead! He treats you like a criminal! He understands nothing! And yet it was exactly the same type of cheap quack who first gave you the medicine – and you never knew what it was until too late! (*Passionately.*) I hate doctors! They'll do anything – anything to keep you coming to them. They'll sell their souls! What's more, they'll sell yours, and you never know it till one day you find yourself in hell!

EDMUND. Mama! For God's sake, stop talking.

TYRONE (*shakenly*). Yes, Mary, it's no time –

MARY (*suddenly is overcome by guilty confusion – stammers*). I – Forgive me, dear. You're right. It's useless to be angry now. (*There is again a pause of dead silence. When she speaks again, her face has cleared and is calm, and the quality of uncanny detachment is in her voice and manner.*) I'm going upstairs for a moment, if you'll excuse me. I have to fix my hair. (*She adds smilingly.*) That is if I can find my glasses. I'll be right down.

TYRONE (*as she starts through the doorway – pleading and rebuking*). Mary!

MARY (*turns to stare at him calmly*). Yes, dear? What is it?

TYRONE (*helplessly*). Nothing.

MARY (*with a strange derisive smile*). You're welcome to come up and watch me if you're so suspicious.

TYRONE. As if that could do any good! You'd only postpone it. And I'm not your jailor. This isn't a prison.

MARY. No. I know you can't help thinking it's a home. (*She adds quickly with a detached contrition.*) I'm sorry, dear. I don't mean to be bitter. It's not your fault.

She turns and disappears through the back parlour. The three in the room remain silent. It is as if they were waiting until she got upstairs before speaking.

JAMIE (*cynically brutal*). Another shot in the arm!

EDMUND (*angrily*). Cut out that kind of talk!

TYRONE. Yes! Hold your foul tongue and your rotten Broadway loafer's lingo! Have you no pity or decency? (*Losing his temper.*) You ought to be kicked out in the gutter! But if I did it, you know damned well who'd weep and plead for you, and excuse you and complain till I let you come back.

JAMIE (*a spasm of pain crosses his face*). Christ, don't I know that? No pity? I have all the pity in the world for her. I understand what a hard game to beat she's up against – which is more than you ever have! My lingo didn't mean I had no feeling. I was merely putting bluntly what we all know, and have to live with now, again. (*Bitterly.*) The cures are no damned good except for a while. The truth is there is no cure and we've been saps to hope – (*Cynically.*) They never come back!

EDMUND (*scornfully parodying his brother's cynicism*). They never come back! Everything is in the bag! It's all a frame-up! We're all fall guys and suckers and we can't beat the game! (*Disdainfully.*) Christ, if I felt the way you do – !

JAMIE (*stung for a moment – then shrugging his shoulders, dryly*). I thought you did. Your poetry isn't very cheery. Nor the stuff you read and claim you admire. (*He indicates the smart bookcase at rear.*) Your pet with the unpronounceable name, for example.

EDMUND. Nietzche. You don't know what you're talking about. You haven't read him.

JAMIE. Enough to know it's a lot of bunk!

TYRONE. Shut up, both of you! There's little choice between the philosophy you learned from Broadway loafers, and the one Edmund got from his books. They're both rotten to the core. You've both flouted the faith you were born and brought up in – the one true faith of the Catholic Church – and your denial has brought nothing but self-destruction!

His two sons stare at him contemptuously. They forget their quarrel and are as one against him on this issue.

EDMUND. That's the bunk, Papa!

JAMIE. We don't pretend, at any rate. (*Caustically.*). I don't notice you've worn any holes in the knees of your pants going to Mass.

TYRONE. It's true I'm a bad Catholic in the observance, God forgive me. But I believe! (*Angrily.*) And you're a liar! I may not go to church but every night and morning of my life I get on my knees and pray!

EDMUND (*bitingly*). Did you pray for Mama?

TYRONE. I did. I've prayed to God these many years for her.

EDMUND. Then Nietzche must be right. (*He quotes from Thus Spake Zarathustra.*) 'God is dead: of His pity for man hath God died.'

TYRONE (*ignores this*). If your mother had prayed, too – She hasn't denied her faith, but she's forgotten it, until now there's no strength of the spirit left in her to fight against her curse. (*Then dully resigned.*) But what's the good of talk? We've lived with this before and now we must again. There's no help for it. (*Bitterly.*) Only I wish she hadn't led me to hope this time. By God, I never will again!

EDMUND. That's a rotten thing to say, Papa! (*Defiantly.*) Well, I'll hope! She's just started. It can't have got a hold on her yet. She can still stop. I'm going to talk to her.

JAMIE (*shrugs his shoulders*). You can't talk to her now. She'll listen but she won't listen. She'll be here but she won't be here. You know the way she gets.

TYRONE. Yes, that's the way the poison acts on her always. Every day from now on, there'll be the same drifting away from us until by the end of each night –

EDMUND (*miserably*). Cut it out, Papa! (*He jumps up from his chair.*) I'm going to get dressed. (*Bitterly, as he goes.*) I'll make so much noise she can't suspect I've come to spy on her. (*He disappears through the front parlour and can be heard stamping noisily upstairs.*)

JAMIE (*after a pause*). What did Doc Hardy say about the Kid?

TYRONE (*dully*). It's what you thought. He's got consumption.

JAMIE. God damn it!

TYRONE. There's no possible doubt, he said.

JAMIE. He'll have to go to a sanatorium.

TYRONE. Yes, and the sooner the better, Hardy said, for him and everyone around him. He claims that in six months to a year Edmund will be cured, if he obeys orders. (*He sighs – gloomily and resentfully.*) I never thought a child of mine – It doesn't come from my side of the family. There wasn't one of us that didn't have lungs as strong as an ox.

JAMIE. Who gives a damn about that part of it! Where does Hardy want to send him?

TYRONE. That's what I'm to see him about.

JAMIE. Well, for God's sake, pick out a good place and not some cheap dump!

TYRONE (*stung*). I'll send him wherever Hardy thinks best!

JAMIE. Well, don't give Hardy your old over-the-hills-to-the-poorhouse song about taxes and mortgages.

TYRONE. I'm no millionaire who can throw money away! Why shouldn't I tell Hardy the truth?

JAMIE. Because he'll think you want him to pick a cheap dump, and because he'll know it isn't the truth – especially if he hears afterwards you've seen McGuire and let that flannel-mouth, gold-brick merchant sting you with another piece of bum property!

TYRONE (*furiously*). Keep your nose out of my business!

JAMIE. This is Edmund's business. What I'm afraid of is, with your Irish bog-trotter idea that consumption is fatal, you'll figure it would be a waste of money to spend any more than you can help.

TYRONE. You liar!

JAMIE. All right. Prove I'm a liar. That's what I want. That's why I brought it up.

TYRONE (*his rage still smouldering*). I have every hope Edmund will be cured. And keep your dirty tongue off Ireland! You're a fine one to sneer, with the map of it on your face!

JAMIE. Not after I wash my face. (*Then before his father can react to this insult to the Old Sod, he adds dryly, shrugging his shoulders.*) Well, I've said all I have to say. It's up to you. (*Abruptly.*) What do you want me to do this afternoon, now you're going uptown? I've done all I can do on the hedge until you cut more of it. You don't want me to go ahead with your clipping, I know that.

TYRONE. No. You'd get it crooked, as you get everything else.

JAMIE. Then I'd better go uptown with Edmund. The bad news coming on top of what's happened to Mama may hit him hard.

TYRONE (*forgetting his quarrel*). Yes, go with him, Jamie. Keep up his spirits, if you can. (*He adds caustically.*) If you can without making it an excuse to get drunk!

JAMIE. What would I use for money? The last I heard they were still selling booze, not giving it away. (*He starts for the front-parlour doorway.*) I'll get dressed.

He stops in the doorway as he sees his mother approaching from the hall, and moves aside to let her come in. Her eyes look brighter, and her manner is more detached. This change becomes more marked as the scene goes on.

MARY (*vaguely*). You haven't seen my glasses anywhere, have you, Jamie?

She doesn't look at him. He glances away, ignoring her question but she doesn't seem to expect an answer. She comes forward, addressing her husband without looking at him.

You haven't seen them, have you, James?

Behind her JAMIE disappears through the front parlour.

TYRONE (*turns to look out of the screen door*). No, Mary.

MARY. What's the matter with Jamie? Have you been nagging at him again? You shouldn't treat him with such contempt all the time. He's not to blame. If he'd been brought up in a real home, I'm sure he would have been different. (*She comes to the windows at right – lightly.*) You're not much of a weather prophet, dear. See how hazy it's getting. I can hardly see the other shore.

TYRONE (*trying to speak naturally*). Yes, I spoke too soon. We're in for another night of fog, I'm afraid.

MARY. Oh, well, I won't mind it tonight.

TYRONE. No, I don't imagine you will, Mary.

MARY (*flashes a glance at him – after a pause*). I don't see Jamie going down to the hedge. Where did he go?

TYRONE. He's going with Edmund to the Doctor's. He went up to change his clothes. (*Then, glad of an excuse to leave her.*) I'd better do the same or I'll be late for my appointment at the Club.

He makes a move toward the front-parlour doorway, but with a swift impulsive movement she reaches out and clasps his arm.

MARY (*a note of pleading in her voice*). Don't go yet, dear. I don't want to be alone. (*Hastily.*) I mean, you have plenty of time. You know you boast you can dress in one-tenth the time it takes the boys. (*Vaguely.*) There is something I wanted to say. What is it? I've forgotten. I'm glad Jamie is going uptown. You didn't give him any money, I hope.

TYRONE. I did not.

MARY. He'd only spend it on drink and you know what a vile, poisonous tongue he has when he's drunk. Not that I would mind anything he said tonight, but he always manages to drive you into a rage, especially if you're drunk, too, as you will be.

TYRONE (*resentfully*). I won't. I never get drunk.

MARY (*teasing indifferently*). Oh, I'm sure you'll hold it well. You always have. It's hard for a stranger to tell, but after thirty-five years of marriage –

TYRONE. I've never missed a performance in my life. That's the proof! (*Then bitterly.*) If I did get drunk it is not you who should blame me. No man has ever had a better reason.

MARY. Reason? What reason? You always drink too much when you go to the Club, don't you? Particularly when you meet

McGuire. He sees to that. Don't think I'm finding fault, dear. You must do as you please. I won't mind.

TYRONE. I know you won't. (*He turns toward the front parlour, anxious to escape.*) I've got to get dressed.

MARY (*again she reaches out and grasps his arm – pleadingly*). No, please wait a little while, dear. At least, until one of the boys comes down. You will all be leaving me so soon.

TYRONE (*with bitter sadness*). It's you who are leaving us, Mary.

MARY. I? That's a silly thing to say, James. How could I leave? There is nowhere I could go. Who would I go to see? I have no friends.

TYRONE. It's your own fault – (*He stops and sighs helplessly – persuasively.*) There's surely one thing you can do this afternoon that will be good for you, Mary. Take a drive in the automobile. Get away from the house. Get a little sun and fresh air. (*Injuredly.*) I bought the automobile for you. You know I don't like the damned things. I'd rather walk any day, or take a trolley. (*With growing resentment.*) I had it here waiting for you when you came back from the sanatorium. I hoped it would give you pleasure and distract your mind. You used to ride in it every day, but you've hardly used it at all lately. I paid a lot of money I couldn't afford, and there's the chauffeur I have to board and lodge and pay high wages whether he drives you or not. (*Bitterly.*) Waste! The same old waste that will land me in the poorhouse in my old age! What good did it do you? I might as well have thrown the money out of the window.

MARY (*with detached calm*). Yes, it was a waste of money, James. You shouldn't have bought a secondhand automobile. You were swindled again as you always are, because you insist on secondhand bargains in everything.

TYRONE. It's one of the best makes! Everyone says it's better than any of the new ones!

MARY (*ignoring this*). It was another waste to hire Smythe, who was only a helper in a garage and had never been a chauffeur. Oh, I realize his wages are less than a real chauffeur's, but he more than makes up for that, I'm sure, by the graft he gets from the garage on repair bills. Something is always wrong. Smythe sees to that, I'm afraid.

TYRONE. I don't believe it! He may not be a fancy millionaire's flunkey but he's honest! You're as bad as Jamie, suspecting everyone!

MARY. You mustn't be offended, dear. I wasn't offended when you gave me the automobile. I knew you didn't mean to humiliate me. I knew that was the way you had to do everything. I was grateful and touched. I knew buying the car was a hard thing for you to do, and it proved how much you loved me, in your way, especially when you couldn't really believe it would do me any good.

TYRONE. Mary! (*He suddenly hugs her to him – brokenly*). Dear Mary! For the love of God, for my sake and the boys' sake and your own, won't you stop now?

MARY (*stammers in guilty confusion for a second*). I – James! Please! (*Her strange, stubborn defence comes back instantly.*) Stop what? What are you talking about?

He lets his arm fall to his side brokenly. She impulsively puts her arm around him.

James! We've loved each other! We always will! Let's remember only that, and not try to understand what we cannot understand, or help things that cannot be helped – the things life has done to us we cannot excuse or explain.

TYRONE (*as if he hadn't heard – bitterly*). You won't even try?

MARY (*her arms drop hopelessly and she turns away – with detachment*). Try to go for a drive this afternoon, you mean? Why, yes, if you wish me to, although it makes me feel lonelier than if I stayed here. There is no one I can invite to drive with me, and I never know where to tell Smythe to go. If there was a friend's house where I could drop in and laugh and gossip awhile. But, of course, there isn't. There never has been. (*Her manner becoming more and more remote.*) At the Convent I had so many friends. Girls whose families lived in lovely homes. I used to visit them and they'd visit me in my father's home. But, naturally, after I married an actor – you know how actors were considered in those days – a lot of them gave me the cold shoulder. And then, right after we were married, there was the scandal of that woman who had been your mistress, suing you. From then on, all my old friends either pitied me or cut me dead. I hated the ones who cut me much less than the pitiers.

TYRONE (*with guilty resentment*). For God's sake, don't dig up what's long forgotten. If you're that far gone in the past already, when it's only the beginning of the afternoon, what will you be tonight?

MARY (*stares at him defiantly now*). Come to think of it, I do have to drive uptown. There's something I must get at the drugstore.

TYRONE (*bitterly scornful*). Leave it to you to have some of the stuff hidden, and prescriptions for more! I hope you'll lay in a good stock ahead so we'll never have another night like the one when you screamed for it, and ran out of the house in your nightdress half crazy, to try and throw yourself off the dock!

MARY (*tries to ignore this*). I have to get tooth powder and toilet soap and cold cream – (*She breaks down pitiably.*) James! You mustn't remember! You mustn't humiliate me so!

TYRONE. (*ashamed*). I'm sorry. Forgive me, Mary!

MARY (*defensively detached again*). It doesn't matter. Nothing like that ever happened. You must have dreamed it.

He stares at her hopelessly. Her voice seems to drift farther and farther away.

I was so healthy before Edmund was born. You remember, James. There wasn't a nerve in my body. Even travelling with you season after season, with week after week of one-night stands, in trains without Pullmans, in dirty rooms of filthy hotels, eating bad food, bearing children in hotel rooms, I still kept healthy. But bearing Edmund was the last straw. I was so sick afterwards, and that ignorant quack of a cheap hotel doctor – All he knew was I was in pain. It was easy for him to stop the pain.

TYRONE. Mary! For God's sake, forget the past!

MARY (*with strange objective calm*). Why? How can I? The past is the present, isn't it? It's the future, too. We all try to lie out of that but life won't let us. (*Going on.*) I blame only myself. I swore after Eugene died I would never have another baby. I was to blame for his death. If I hadn't left him with my mother to join you on the road, because you wrote telling me you missed me and were so lonely, Jamie would never have been allowed, when he still had measles, to go in the baby's room. (*Her face hardening.*) I've always believed Jamie did it on purpose. He was jealous of the baby. He hated him. (*As TYRONE starts to protest.*) Oh, I know Jamie was only seven, but he was never stupid. He'd been warned it might kill the baby. He knew. I've never been able to forgive him for that.

TYRONE (*with bitter sadness*). Are you back with Eugene now? Can't you let our dead baby rest in peace?

MARY (*as if she hadn't heard him*). It was my fault. I should have insisted on staying with Eugene and not have let you persuade me to join you, just because I loved you. Above all, I shouldn't have let you insist I have another baby to take Eugene's place, because you thought that would make me forget his death. I knew from experience by then that children should have homes to be born in, if they are to be good children, and women need homes, if they are to be good mothers. I was afraid all the time I carried Edmund. I knew something terrible would happen. I knew I'd proved by the way I'd left Eugene that I wasn't worthy to have another baby, and that God would punish me if I did. I never should have borne Edmund.

TYRONE (*with an uneasy glance through the front parlour*). Mary! Be careful with your talk. If he heard you he might think you never wanted him. He's feeling bad enough already without –

MARY (*violently*). It's a lie! I did want him! More than anything in the world! You don't understand! I meant, for his sake. He has never been happy. He never will be. Nor healthy. He was born nervous and too sensitive, and that's my fault. And now, ever since he's been so sick I've kept remembering Eugene and my father and I've been so frightened and guilty – (*Then, catching herself, with an instant change to stubborn denial.*) Oh, I know it's foolish to imagine dreadful things when there's no reason for it. After all, everyone has colds and gets over them.

TYRONE *stares at her and sighs helplessly. He turns away toward the front parlour and sees* EDMUND *coming down the stairs in the hall.*

TYRONE (*sharply, in a low voice*). Here's Edmund. For God's sake try and be yourself – at least until he goes! You can do that much for him!

He waits, forcing his face into a pleasantly paternal expression. She waits frightenedly, seized again by a nervous panic, her hands fluttering over the bosom of her dress, up to her throat and hair, with a distracted aimlessness. Then, as EDMUND *approaches the doorway, she cannot face him. She goes swiftly away to the windows at left and stares out with her back to the front parlour.* EDMUND *enters. He has changed to a ready-made blue serge suit, high stiff collar and tie, black shoes.*

(*With an actor's heartiness.*) Well! You look spick and span. I'm on my way up to change, too. (*He starts to pass him.*)

EDMUND (*dryly*). Wait a minute, Papa. I hate to bring up disagreeable topics, but there's the matter of carfare. I'm broke.

TYRONE (*starts automatically on a customary lecture*). You'll always be broke until you learn the value – (*Checks himself guiltily, looking at his son's sick face with worried pity.*) But you've been learning, lad. You worked hard before you took ill. You've done splendidly. I'm proud of you.

He pulls out a small roll of bills from his pants pocket and carefully selects one. EDMUND takes it. He glances at it and his face expresses astonishment. His father again reacts customarily – sarcastically.

Thank you. (*He quotes.*) 'How sharper than a serpent's tooth it is –'

EDMUND. 'To have a thankless child.' I know. Give me a chance, Papa. I'm knocked speechless. This isn't a dollar. It's a ten spot.

TYRONE (*embarrassed by his generosity*). Put it in your pocket. You'll probably meet some of your friends uptown and you can't hold your end up and be sociable with nothing in your jeans.

EDMUND. You meant it? Gosh, thank you, Papa. (*He is genuinely pleased and grateful for a moment – then he stares at his father's face with uneasy suspicion.*) But why all of a sudden–? (*Cynically.*) Did Doc Hardy tell you I was going to die? (*Then he sees his father is bitterly hurt.*) No! That's a rotten crack. I was only kidding, Papa. (*He puts his arm around his father impulsively and gives him an affectionate hug.*) I'm very grateful. Honest, Papa.

TYRONE (*touched, returns his hug*). You're welcome, lad.

MARY (*suddenly turns to them in a confused panic of frightened anger*). I won't have it! (*She stamps her foot.*) Do you hear, Edmund! Such morbid nonsense! Saying you're going to die! It's the books you read! Nothing but sadness and death! Your father shouldn't allow you to have them. And some of the poems you've written yourself are even worse! You'd think you didn't want to live! A boy of your age with everything before him! It's just a pose you get out of books! You're not really sick at all!

TYRONE. Mary! Hold your tongue!

MARY (*instantly changing to a detached tone*). But, James, it's absurd of Edmund to be so gloomy and make such a great to-do about nothing. (*Turning to* EDMUND *but avoiding his eyes – teasingly affectionate.*) Never mind, dear. I'm on to you. (*She comes to him.*)

You want to be petted and spoiled and made a fuss over, isn't that it? You're still such a baby.

She puts her arm around him and hugs him. He remains rigid and unyielding. Her voice begins to tremble.

But please don't carry it too far. Don't say horrible things. I know it's foolish to take them seriously, but I can't help it. You've got me – so frightened.

She breaks and hides her face on his shoulder, sobbing. EDMUND *is moved in spite of himself. He pats her shoulder with an awkward tenderness.*

EDMUND. Don't, mother. (*His eyes meet his father's.*)

TYRONE (*huskily – clutching at hopeless hope*). Maybe if you asked your mother now what you said you were going to – (*He fumbles with his watch.*) By God, look at the time! I'll have to shake a leg.

He hurries away through the front parlour. MARY *lifts her head. Her manner is again one of detached motherly solicitude. She seems to have forgotten the tears which are still in her eyes.*

MARY. How do you feel, dear? (*She feels his forehead.*) Your head is a little hot, but that's just from going out in the sun. You look ever so much better than you did this morning. (*Taking his hand.*) Come and sit down. You musn't stand on your feet so much. You must learn to husband your strength. (*She gets him to sit and she sits sideways on the arm of his chair, an arm around his shoulder, so he cannot meet her eyes.*)

EDMUND (*starts to blurt out the appeal he now feels is quite hopeless*). Listen, Mama –

MARY (*interrupting quickly*). Now, now! Don't talk. Lean back and rest. (*Persuasively.*) You know, I think it would be much better for you if you stayed home this afternoon and let me take care of you. It's such a tiring trip uptown in the dirty old trolley on a day like this. I'm sure you'd be much better off here with me.

EDMUND (*dully*). You forget I have an appointment with Hardy. (*Trying again to get his appeal started.*) Listen, Mama –

MARY (*quickly*). You can telephone and say you don't feel well enough. (*Excitedly.*) It's simply a waste of time and money seeing him. He'll only tell you some lie. He'll pretend he's found something serious the matter because that's his bread and butter. (*She gives a hard sneering little laugh.*) The old idiot! All he knows about medicine is to look solemn and preach will-power!

EDMUND (*trying to catch her eyes*). Mama! Please listen! I want to ask you something! You – you're only just started. You can still stop. You've got the will-power! We'll all help you. I'll do anything! Won't you, Mama?

MARY (*stammers pleadingly*). Please don't – talk about things you don't understand!

EDMUND (*dully*). All right, I give up. I knew it was no use.

MARY (*in blank denial now*). Anyway, I don't know what you're referring to. But I do know you should be the last one – Right after I returned from the sanatorium, you began to be ill. The doctor there had warned me I must have peace at home with nothing to upset me, and all I've done is worry about you. (*Then distractedly.*) But that's no excuse! I'm only trying to explain. It's not an excuse! (*She hugs him to her – pleadingly.*) Promise me, dear, you won't believe I made you an excuse.

EDMUND (*bitterly*). What else can I believe?

MARY (*slowly takes her arm away – her manner remote and objective again*). Yes, I suppose you can't help suspecting that.

EDMUND (*ashamed but still bitter*). What do you expect?

MARY. Nothing, I don't blame you. How could you believe me – when I can't believe myself? I've become such a liar. I never lied about anything once upon a time. Now I have to lie, especially to myself. But how can you understand, when I don't myself. I've never understood anything about it, except that one day long ago I found I could no longer call my soul my own. (*She pauses – then lowering her voice to a strange tone of whispered confidence.*) But some day, dear, I will find it again – some day when you're all well, and I see you healthy and happy and successful, and I don't have to feel guilty any more – some day when the Blessed Virgin Mary forgives me and gives me back the faith in Her love and pity I used to have in my convent days, and I can pray to Her again – when She sees no one in the world can believe in me even for a moment any more, then She will believe in me, and with Her help it will be so easy. I will hear myself scream with agony, and at the same time I will laugh because I will be so sure of myself. (*Then as EDMUND remains hopelessly silent, she adds sadly.*) Of course, you can't believe that, either. (*She rises from the arm of his chair and goes to stare out of the windows at right with her back to him – casually.*) Now I think of it, you might as well go uptown. I

forgot I'm taking a drive. I have to go to the drugstore. You
would hardly want to go there with me. You'd be so ashamed.

EDMUND (*brokenly*). Mama! Don't!

MARY. I suppose you'll divide that ten dollars your father gave
you with Jamie. You always divide with each other, don't you?
Like good sports. Well, I know what he'll do with his share. Get
drunk someplace where he can be with the only kind of woman
he understands or likes. (*She turns to him, pleading frightenedly.*)
Edmund! Promise me you won't drink! It's so dangerous! You
know Doctor Hardy told you – .

EDMUND (*bitterly*). I thought he was an old idiot.

MARY (*pitifully*). Edmund!

JAMIE'*s voice is heard from the front hall.*

JAMIE. Come on, Kid, let's beat it.

MARY'*s manner at once becomes detached again.*

MARY. Go on, Edmund. Jamie's waiting. (*She goes to the front-
parlour doorway.*) There comes your father downstairs, too.

TYRONE'*s voice calls.*

TYRONE. Come on, Edmund.

MARY (*kisses him with detached affection*). Goodbye, dear. If you're
coming home for dinner, try not to be late. And tell your
father. You know what Bridget is.

He turns and hurries away. TYRONE *calls from the hall.*

TYRONE. Goodbye, Mary.

JAMIE. Goodbye, Mama.

MARY (*calls back*). Goodbye.

*The front screen door is heard closing after them. She comes and stands
by the table, one hand drumming on it, the other fluttering up to pat
her hair.*

*She stares about the room with frightened, forsaken eyes and whispers to
herself.*

It's so lonely here. (*Then her face hardens into bitter self-contempt.*)
You're lying to yourself again. You wanted to get rid of them.
Their contempt and disgust aren't pleasant company. You're
glad they're gone. (*She gives a little despairing laugh.*) Then
Mother of God, why do I feel so lonely?

ACT THREE

Scene. The same. It is around half-past six in the evening. Dusk is gathering in the living-room, an early dusk due to the fog which has rolled in from the Sound and is like a white curtain drawn down outside the windows. From a lighthouse beyond the harbour's mouth, a foghorn is heard at regular intervals, moaning like a mournful whale in labour, and from the harbour itself, intermittently, comes the warning ringing of bells on yachts at anchor.

The tray with the bottle of whiskey, glasses, and pitcher of ice water is on the table, as it was in the pre-luncheon scene of the previous act.

MARY and the second girl, CATHLEEN, are discovered. The latter is standing at left of table. She holds an empty whiskey glass in her hand as if she'd forgotten she had it. She shows the effects of drink. Her stupid, good-humoured face wears a pleased and flattered simper.

MARY is paler than before and her eyes shine with unnatural brilliance. The strange detachment in her manner has intensified. She has hidden deeper within herself and found refuge and release in a dream where present reality is but an appearance to be accepted and dismissed unfeelingly – even with a hard cynicism – or entirely ignored. There is at times an uncanny gay, free youthfulness in her manner, as if in spirit she were released to become again, simply and without self-consciousness, the naïve, happy, chattering schoolgirl of her convent days. She wears the dress into which she had changed for her drive to town, a simple, fairly expensive affair, which would be extremely becoming if it were not for the careless, almost slovenly way she wears it. Her hair is no longer fastidiously in place. It has a slightly dishevelled, lopsided look. She talks to CATHLEEN with a confiding familiarity, as if the second girl were an old, intimate friend. As the curtain rises, she is standing by the screen door looking out. A moan of the foghorn is heard.

MARY (*amused – girlishly*). That foghorn! Isn't it awful, Cathleen?

CATHLEEN (*talks more familiarly than usual but never with intentional impertinence because she sincerely likes her mistress*). It is indeed, Ma'am. It's like a banshee.

MARY (*goes on as if she hadn't heard. In nearly all the following dialogue there is a feeling that she has CATHLEEN with her merely as an excuse to keep talking*). I don't mind it tonight. Last night it drove me crazy. I lay awake worrying until I couldn't stand it any more.

CATHLEEN. Bad cess to it. I was scared out of my wits riding back from town. I thought that ugly monkey, Smythe, would drive us in a ditch or against a tree. You couldn't see your hand in front of you. I'm glad you had me sit in back with you, Ma'am. If I'd been in front with that monkey – He can't keep his dirty hands to himself. Give him a chance and he's pinching me on the leg or you-know-where – asking your pardon, Ma'am, but it's true.

MARY (*dreamily*). It wasn't the fog I minded, Cathleen. I really love fog.

CATHLEEN. They say it's good for the complexion.

MARY. It hides you from the world and the world from you. You feel that everything has changed, and nothing is what it seemed to be. No one can find or touch you any more.

CATHLEEN. I wouldn't care so much if Smythe was a fine, handsome man like some chauffeurs I've seen – I mean, if it was all in fun, for I'm a decent girl. But for a shrivelled runt like Smythe – ! I've told him, you must think I'm hard up that I'd notice a monkey like you. I've warned him, one day I'll give him a clout that'll knock him into next week. And so I will!

MARY. It's the foghorn I hate. It won't let you alone. It keeps reminding you, and warning you, and calling you back. (*She smiles strangely.*) But it can't tonight. It's just an ugly sound. It doesn't remind me of anything. (*She gives a teasing, girlish laugh.*) Except, perhaps, Mr Tyrone's snores. I've always had such fun teasing him about it. He has snored ever since I can remember, especially when he's had too much to drink, and yet he's like a child, he hates to admit it. (*She laughs, coming to the table.*) Well, I suppose I snore at times, too, and I don't like to admit it. So I have no right to make fun of him, have I? (*She sits in the rocker at right of table.*)

CATHLEEN. Ah, sure, everybody healthy snores. It's a sign of sanity, they say. (*Then, worriedly.*) What time is it, Ma'am? I ought to go back in the kitchen. The damp is in Bridget's rheumatism and she's like a raging divil. She'll bite my head off. (*She puts her glass on the table and makes a movement toward the back parlour.*)

MARY (*with a flash of apprehension*). No, don't go, Cathleen. I don't want to be alone, yet.

CATHLEEN. You won't be for long. The Master and the boys will be home soon.

MARY. I doubt if they'll come back for dinner. They have too good an excuse to remain in the bar-rooms where they feel at home.

CATHLEEN *stares at her, stupidly puzzled.* MARY *goes on smilingly.*

Don't worry about Bridget. I'll tell her I kept you with me, and you can take a big drink of whiskey to her when you go. She won't mind then.

CATHLEEN (*grins – at her ease again*). No, Ma'am. That's the one thing can make her cheerful. She loves her drop.

MARY. Have another drink yourself, if you wish, Cathleen.

CATHLEEN. I don't know if I'd better, Ma'am. I can feel what I've had already. (*Reaching for the bottle.*) Well, maybe one more won't harm. (*She pours a drink.*) Here's your good health, Ma'am. (*She drinks without bothering about a chaser.*)

MARY (*dreamily*). I really did have a good health once, Cathleen. But that was long ago.

CATHLEEN (*worried again*). The Master's sure to notice what's gone from the bottle. He has the eye of a hawk for that.

MARY (*amusedly*). Oh, we'll play Jamie's trick on him. Just measure a few drinks of water and pour them in.

CATHLEEN (*does this – with a silly giggle*). God save me, it'll be half water. He'll know by the taste.

MARY (*indifferently*). No, by the time he comes home he'll be too drunk to tell the difference. He has such a good excuse, he believes, to drown his sorrows.

CATHLEEN (*philosophically*). Well, it's a good man's failing. I wouldn't give a trauneen for a teetotaller. They've no high spirits. (*Then, stupidly puzzled.*) Good excuse? You mean Master Edmund, Ma'am? I can tell the Master is worried about him.

MARY (*stiffens defensively – but in a strange way the reaction has a mechanical quality, as if it did not penetrate to real emotion*). Don't be silly, Cathleen. Why should he be? A touch of grippe is nothing. And Mr Tyrone never is worried about anything, except money and property and the fear he'll end his days in poverty. I mean, deeply worried. Because he cannot really understand anything else. (*She gives a little laugh of detached, affectionate amusement.*) My husband is a very peculiar man, Cathleen.

CATHLEEN (*vaguely resentful*). Well, he's a fine, handsome, kind gentleman just the same, Ma'am. Never mind his weakness.

MARY. Oh, I don't mind. I've loved him dearly for thirty-six years. That proves I know he's lovable at heart and can't help being what he is, doesn't it?

CATHLEEN (*hazily reassured*). That's right, Ma'am. Love him dearly, for any fool can see he worships the ground you walk on. (*Fighting the effect of her last drink and trying to be soberly conversational.*) Speaking of acting, Ma'am, how is it you never went on the stage?

MARY (*resentfully*). I? What put that absurd notion in your head? I was brought up in a respectable home and educated in the best convent in the Middle West. Before I met Mr Tyrone I hardly knew there was such a thing as a theatre. I was a very pious girl. I even dreamed of becoming a nun. I've never had the slightest desire to be an actress.

CATHLEEN (*bluntly*) Well, I can't imagine you a holy nun, Ma'am. Sure, you never darken the door of a church, God forgive you.

MARY (*ignores this*). I've never felt at home in the theatre. Even though Mr Tyrone has made me go with him on all his tours, I've had little to do with the people in his company, or with anyone on the stage. Not that I have anything against them. They have always been kind to me, and I to them. But I've never felt at home with them. Their life is not my life. It has always stood between me and – (*She gets up – abruptly.*) But let's not talk of old things that couldn't be helped. (*She goes to the porch door and stares out.*) How thick the fog is. I can't see the road. All the people in the world could pass by and I would never know. I wish it was always that way. It's getting dark already. It will soon be night, thank goodness. (*She turns back – vaguely.*) It was kind of you to keep me company this afternoon, Cathleen. I would have been lonely driving uptown alone.

CATHLEEN. Sure, wouldn't I rather ride in a fine automobile than stay here and listen to Bridget's lies about her relations? It was like a vacation, Ma'am. (*She pauses – then stupidly.*) There was only one thing I didn't like.

MARY (*vaguely*). What was that, Cathleen?

CATHLEEN. The way the man in the drugstore acted when I took in the prescription for you. (*Indignantly*.) The impidence of him!

MARY (*with stubborn blankness*). What are you talking about? What drugstore? What prescription? (*Then hastily, as* CATHLEEN *stares in stupid amazement*.) Oh, of course, I'd forgotten. The medicine for the rheumatism in my hands. What did the man say? (*Then with indifference*.) Not that it matters, as long as he filled the prescription.

CATHLEEN. It mattered to me, then! I'm not used to being treated like a thief. He gave me a long look and says insultingly, 'Where did you get hold of this?' and I says, 'It's none of your damned business, but if you must know, it's for the lady I work for, Mrs Tyrone, who's sitting out in the automobile.' That shut him up quick. He gave a look out at you and said, 'Oh,' and went to get the medicine.

MARY (*vaguely*). Yes, he knows me. (*She sits in the armchair at right rear of table. She adds in a calm, detached voice*.) I have to take it because there is no other that can stop the pain – *all* the pain – I mean, in my hands. (*She raises her hands and regards them with melancholy sympathy. There is no tremor in them now*.) Poor hands! You'd never believe it, but they were once one of my good points, along with my hair and eyes, and I had a fine figure, too. (*Her tone has become more and more far-off and dreamy*.) They were a musician's hands. I used to love the piano. I worked so hard at my music in the Convent – if you can call it work when you do something you love. Mother Elizabeth and my music teacher both said I had more talent than any student they remembered. My father paid for special lessons. He spoiled me. He would do anything I asked. He would have sent me to Europe to study after I graduated from the Convent. I might have gone – if I hadn't fallen in love with Mr Tyrone. Or I might have become a nun. I had two dreams. To be a nun, that was the more beautiful one. To become a concert pianist, that was the other.

She pauses, regarding her hands fixedly. CATHLEEN *blinks her eyes to fight off drowsiness and a tipsy feeling.*

I haven't touched a piano in so many years. I couldn't play with such crippled fingers, even if I wanted to. For a time after my marriage I tried to keep up my music. But it was hopeless.

One-night stands, cheap hotels, dirty trains, bearing children, never having a home – (*She stares at her hands with fascinated disgust.*) See, Cathleen, how ugly they are! So maimed and crippled! You would think they'd been through some horrible accident! (*She gives a strange little laugh.*) So they have, come to think of it. (*She suddenly thrusts her hands behind her back.*) I won't look at them. They're worse than the foghorn for reminding me – (*Then with a defiant self-assurance.*) But even they can't touch me now. (*She brings her hands from behind her back and deliberately stares at them – calmly.*) They're far away. I see them, but the pain has gone.

CATHLEEN (*stupidly puzzled*). You've taken some of the medicine? It made you act funny, Ma'am. If I didn't know better, I'd think you'd a drop taken.

MARY (*dreamily*). It kills the pain. You go back until at last you are beyond its reach. Only the past when you were happy is real. (*She pauses – then as if her words had been an evocation which called back happiness she changes in her whole manner and facial expression. She looks younger. There is a quality of an innocent convent girl about her, and she smiles shyly.*) If you think Mr Tyrone is handsome now, Cathleen, you should have seen him when I first met him. He had the reputation of being one of the best-looking men in the country. The girls in the Convent who had seen him act, or seen his photographs, used to rave about him. He was a great matinée idol then, you know. Women used to wait at the stage door just to see him come out. You can imagine how excited I was, when my father wrote me he and James Tyrone had become friends, and that I was to meet him when I came home for Easter vacation. I showed the letter to all the girls, and how envious they were! My father took me to see him at first. It was a play about the French Revolution and the leading part was a nobleman. I couldn't take my eyes off him. I wept when he was thrown in prison – and then was so mad at myself because I was afraid my eyes and nose would be red. My father said we'd go backstage to his dressing-room right after the play, and so we did. (*She gives a little excited, shy laugh.*) I was so bashful all I could do was stammer and blush like a little fool. But he didn't seem to think I was a fool. I know he liked me the first moment we were introduced. (*Coquettishly.*) I guess my eyes and nose couldn't have been red, after all. I was really very pretty then, Cathleen. And he was handsomer than my wildest dream, in his make-up and his nobleman's costume that was so becoming to him. He was different from all ordinary men, like someone from another world. At the same time he was simple, and kind and unassuming, not a bit stuck-up or vain. I fell in love right then. So did he, he told me afterwards. I forgot all about becoming a nun or a concert pianist. All I wanted was to be his wife. (*She pauses, staring before her with unnaturally bright, dreamy eyes, and a rapt, tender, girlish smile.*) Thirty-six years ago, but I can see it as clearly as if it were tonight! We've loved each other ever since. And in all those thirty-six years, there has never been a breath of scandal about him. I mean, with any other woman. Not since he met me. That has made me very happy, Cathleen. It has made me forgive so many other things.

CATHLEEN (*fighting tipsy drowsiness – sentimentally*). He's a fine gentleman and you're a lucky lady. (*Then fidgeting.*) Can I take the drink to Bridget, Ma'am? It must be near dinner-time and I ought to be in the kitchen helping her. If she don't get something to quiet her temper, she'll be after me with the cleaver.

MARY (*with a vague exasperation at being brought back from her dream*).

Yes, yes, go. I don't need you now.

CATHLEEN (*with relief*). Thank you, Ma'am. (*She pours out a big drink and starts for the back parlour with it.*) You won't be alone long. The Master and the boys –

MARY (*impatiently*). No, no, they won't come. Tell Bridget I won't wait. You can serve dinner promptly at half-past six. I'm not hungry but I'll sit at the table and we'll get it over with.

CATHLEEN. You ought to eat something, Ma'am. It's a queer medicine if it takes away your appetite.

MARY (*has begun to drift into dreams again – reacts mechanically*). What medicine? I don't know what you mean. (*In dismissal.*) You better take the drink to Bridget.

CATHLEEN. Yes, Ma'am.

She disappears through the back parlour. MARY waits until she hears the pantry door close behind her. Then she settles back in relaxed dreaminess, staring fixedly at nothing. Her arms rest limply along the arms of the chair, her hands with long, warped, swollen-knuckled, sensitive fingers drooping in complete calm. It is growing dark in the room. There is a pause of dead quiet. Then from the world outside comes the melancholy moan of the foghorn, followed by a chorus of

bells, *muffled by the fog, from the anchored craft in the harbour.*
MARY's *face gives no sign she has heard, but her hands jerk and the*
fingers automatically play for a moment on the air. She frowns and
shakes her head mechanically as if a fly had walked across her mind.
She suddenly loses all the girlish quality and is an ageing, cynically
sad, embittered woman.

MARY (*bitterly*). You're a sentimental fool. What is so wonderful
about that first meeting between a silly romantic schoolgirl and
a matinée idol? You were much happier before you knew he
existed, in the Convent when you used to pray to the Blessed
Virgin. (*Longingly.*) If I could only find the faith I lost, so I
could pray again! (*She pauses – then begins to recite the Hail Mary*
in a flat, empty tone.) 'Hail, Mary, full of grace! the Lord is with
Thee; blessed art Thou among women.' (*Sneeringly.*) You expect
the Blessed Virgin to be fooled by a lying dope fiend reciting
words! You can't hide from Her! (*She springs to her feet. Her*
hands fly up to pat her hair distractedly.) I must go upstairs. I
haven't taken enough. When you start again you never know
exactly how much you need. (*She goes toward the front parlour –*
then stops in the doorway as she hears the sound of voices from the
front path. She starts guiltily.) That must be them – (*She hurries*
back to sit down. Her face sets in stubborn defensiveness – resentfully.)
Why are they coming back? They don't want to. And I'd much
rather be alone. (*Suddenly her whole manner changes. She becomes*
pathetically relieved and eager.) Oh, I'm so glad they've come! I've
been so horribly lonely!

The front door is heard closing and TYRONE *calls uneasily from the*
hall.

TYRONE. Are you there, Mary?

The light in the hall is turned on and shines through the front parlour
to fall on MARY.

MARY (*rises from her chair, her face lighting up lovingly – with excited*
eagerness). I'm here, dear. In the living-room. I've been waiting
for you.

TYRONE *comes in through the front parlour.* EDMUND *is behind*
him. TYRONE *has had a lot to drink but beyond a slightly glazed look*
in his eyes and a trace of blur in his speech, he does not show it.
EDMUND *has also had more than a few drinks without much*
apparent effect, except that his sunken cheeks are flushed and his eyes
look bright and feverish. They stop in the doorway to stare appraisingly
at her. What they see fulfils their worst expectations. But for the

moment MARY *is unconscious of their condemning eyes. She kisses her husband and then* EDMUND. *Her manner is unnaturally effusive. They submit shrinkingly. She talks excitedly.*

I'm so happy you've come. I had given up hope. I was so afraid you wouldn't come home. It's such a dismal, foggy evening. It must be much more cheerful in the bar-rooms uptown, where there are people you can talk and joke with. No, don't deny it. I know how you feel. I don't blame you a bit. I'm all the more grateful to you for coming home. I was sitting here so lonely and blue. Come and sit down.

She sits at left rear of table, EDMUND *at left of table, and* TYRONE *in the rocker at right of it.*

Dinner won't be ready for a minute. You're actually a little early. Will wonders never cease? Here's the whiskey, dear. Shall I pour a drink for you? (*Without waiting for a reply she does so.*) And you, Edmund? I don't want to encourage you, but one before dinner, as an appetizer, can't do any harm.

She pours a drink for him. They make no move to take the drinks. She talks on as if unaware of their silence.

Where's Jamie? But, of course, he'll never come home so long as he has the price of a drink left. (*She reaches out and clasps her husband's hand – sadly.*) I'm afraid Jamie has been lost to us for a long time, dear. (*Her face hardens.*) But we mustn't allow him to drag Edmund down with him, as he'd like to do. He's jealous because Edmund has always been the baby – just as he used to be of Eugene. He'll never be content until he makes Edmund as hopeless a failure as he is.

EDMUND (*miserably*). Stop talking, Mama.

TYRONE (*dully*). Yes, Mary, the less you say now – (*Then to* EDMUND, *a bit tipsily.*) All the same there's truth in your mother's warning. Beware of that brother of yours, or he'll poison life for you with his damned sneering serpent's tongue!

EDMUND (*as before*). Oh, cut it out, Papa.

MARY (*goes on as if nothing had been said*). It's hard to believe, seeing Jamie as he is now, that he was ever my baby. Do you remember what a healthy, happy baby he was, James? The one-night stands and filthy trains and cheap hotels and bad food never made him cross or sick. He was always smiling or laughing. He hardly ever cried. Eugene was the same, too, happy and healthy, during the two years he lived before I let him die through my neglect.

TYRONE. Oh, for the love of God! I'm a fool for coming home!

EDMUND. Papa! Shut up!

MARY (*smiles with detached tenderness at* EDMUND). It was Edmund who was the crosspatch when he was little, always getting upset and frightened about nothing at all. (*She pats his hand – teasingly.*) Everyone used to say, dear, you'd cry at the drop of a hat.

EDMUND (*cannot control his bitterness*). Maybe I guessed there was a good reason not to laugh.

TYRONE (*reproving and pitying*). Now, now, lad. You know better than to pay attention –

MARY (*as if she hadn't heard – sadly again*). Who would have thought Jamie would grow up to disgrace us. You remember, James, for years after he went to boarding school, we received such glowing reports. Everyone liked him. All his teachers told us what a fine brain he had, and how easily he learned his lessons. Even after he began to drink and they had to expel him, they wrote us how sorry they were, because he was so likeable and such a brilliant student. They predicted a wonderful future for him if he would only learn to take life seriously. (*She pauses – then adds with a strange, sad detachment.*) It's such a pity. Poor Jamie! It's hard to understand –(*Abruptly a change comes over her. Her face hardens and she stares at her husband with accusing hostility.*) No, it isn't at all. You brought him up to be a boozer. Since he first opened his eyes, he's seen you drinking. Always a bottle on the bureau in the cheap hotel rooms! And if he had a nightmare when he was little, or a stomach-ache, your remedy was to give him a teaspoonful of whiskey to quiet him.

TYRONE (*stung*). So I'm to blame because that lazy hulk has made a drunken loafer of himself? Is that what I came home to listen to? I might have known! When you have the poison in you, you want to blame everyone but yourself!

EDMUND. Papa! You told me not to pay attention. (*Then, resentfully.*) Anyway it's true. You did the same thing with me. I can remember that teaspoonful of booze every time I woke up with a nightmare.

MARY (*in a detached reminiscent tone*). Yes, you were continually having nightmares as a child. You were born afraid. Because I was so afraid to bring you into the world. (*She pauses – then goes on with the same detachment.*) Please don't think I blame your father, Edmund. He didn't know any better. He never went to school after he was ten. His people were the most ignorant kind of poverty-stricken Irish. I'm sure they honestly believed whiskey is the healthiest medicine for a child who is sick or frightened.

TYRONE *is about to burst out in angry defence of his family but* EDMUND *intervenes.*

EDMUND (*sharply*). Papa! (*Changing the subject.*) Are we going to have this drink, or aren't we?

TYRONE (*controlling himself – dully*). You're right. I'm a fool to take notice. (*He picks up his glass listlessly.*) Drink hearty, lad.

EDMUND *drinks but* TYRONE *remains staring at the glass in his hand.* EDMUND *at once realizes how much the whiskey has been watered. He frowns, glancing from the bottle to his mother – starts to say something but stops.*

MARY (*in a changed tone – repentantly*). I'm sorry if I sounded bitter, James. I'm not. It's all so far away. But I did feel a little hurt when you wished you hadn't come home. I was so relieved and happy when you came, and grateful to you. It's very dreary and sad to be here alone in the fog with night falling.

TYRONE (*moved*). I'm glad I came, Mary, when you act like your real self.

MARY. I was so lonesome I kept Cathleen with me just to have someone to talk to. (*Her manner and quality drift back to the shy convent girl again.*) Do you know what I was telling her, dear? About the night my father took me to your dressing-room and I first fell in love with you. Do you remember?

TYRONE (*deeply moved – his voice husky*). Can you think I'd ever forget, Mary?

EDMUND *looks away from them, sad and embarrassed.*

MARY (*tenderly*). No. I know you still love me, James, in spite of everything.

TYRONE (*his face works and he blinks back tears – with quiet intensity*). Yes! As God is my judge! Always and for ever, Mary!

MARY. And I love you, dear, in spite of everything.

There is a pause in which EDMUND *moves embarrassedly. The strange detachment comes over her manner again as if she were speaking impersonally of people seen from a distance.*

But I must confess, James, although I couldn't help loving you, I would never have married you if I'd known you drank so much. I remember the first night your bar-room friends had to help you up to the door of our hotel room, and knocked and then ran away before I came to the door. We were still on our honeymoon, do you remember?

TYRONE (*with guilty vehemence*). I don't remember. It wasn't on our honeymoon! And I never in my life had to be helped to bed, or missed a performance!

MARY (*as though he hadn't spoken*). I had waited in that ugly hotel room hour after hour. I kept making excuses for you. I told myself it must be some business connected with the theatre. I knew so little about the theatre. Then I became terrified. I imagined all sorts of horrible accidents. I got on my knees and prayed that nothing had happened to you – and then they brought you up and left you outside the door. (*She gives a little, sad sigh.*) I didn't know how often that was to happen in the years to come, how many times I was to wait in ugly hotel rooms. I became quite used to it.

EDMUND (*bursts out with a look of accusing hate at his father*). Christ! No wonder – ! (*He controls himself – gruffly.*) When is dinner, Mama? It must be time.

TYRONE (*overwhelmed by shame which he tries to hide, fumbles with his watch*). Yes. It must be. Let's see. (*He stares at his watch without seeing it. Pleadingly.*) Mary! Can't you forget – ?

MARY (*with detached pity*). No, dear. But I forgive. I always forgive you. So don't look so guilty. I'm sorry I remembered out loud. I don't want to be sad, or to make you sad. I want to remember only the happy part of the past. (*Her manner drifts back to the shy, gay convent girl.*) Do you remember our wedding, dear? I'm sure you've completely forgotten what my wedding gown looked like. Men don't notice such things. They don't think they're important. But it was important to me, I can tell you! How I fussed and worried! I was so excited and happy! My father told me to buy anything I wanted and never mind what it cost. The best is none too good, he said. I'm afraid he spoiled me dreadfully. My mother didn't. She was very pious and strict. I think she was a little jealous. She didn't approve of my marrying – especially an actor. I think she hoped I would become a nun. She used to scold my father. She'd grumble, 'You never tell me, never mind what it costs, when I buy anything! You've spoiled that girl so, I pity her husband if she ever marries. She'll expect him to give her the moon. She'll never make a good wife.' (*She laughs affectionately.*) Poor mother! (*She smiles at* TYRONE *with a strange, incongruous coquetry.*) But she was mistaken, wasn't she, James? I haven't been such a bad wife, have I?

TYRONE (*huskily, trying to force a smile*). I'm not complaining, Mary.

MARY (*a shadow of vague guilt crosses her face*). At least, I've loved you dearly, and done the best I could – under the circumstances. (*The shadow vanishes and her shy, girlish expression returns.*) That wedding gown was nearly the death of me and the dressmaker, too! (*She laughs.*) I was so particular. It was never quite good enough. At last she said she refused to touch it any more or she might spoil it, and I made her leave so I could be alone to examine myself in the mirror. I was so pleased and vain. I thought to myself, 'Even if your nose and mouth and ears are a trifle too large, your eyes and hair and figure, and your hands, make up for it. You're just as pretty as any actress he's ever met, and you don't have to use paint.' (*She pauses, wrinkling her brow in an effort of memory.*) Where is my wedding gown now, I wonder? I kept it wrapped up in tissue paper in my trunk. I used to hope I would have a daughter and when it came time for her to marry – She couldn't have bought a lovelier gown, and I knew, James, you'd never tell her, never mind the cost. You'd want her to pick up something at a bargain. It was made of soft, shimmering satin, trimmed with wonderful old duchesse lace, in tiny ruffles around the neck and sleeves, and worked in with the folds that were draped round in a bustle effect at the back. The basque was boned and very tight. I remember I held my breath when it was fitted, so my waist would be as small as possible. My father even let me have duchesse lace on my white satin slippers, and lace with the orange blossoms in my veil. Oh, how I loved that gown! It was so beautiful! Where is it now, I wonder? I used to take it out from time to time when I was lonely, but it always made me cry, so finally a long while ago – (*She wrinkles her forehead again.*) I wonder where I hid it? Probably in one of the old trunks in the attic. Some day I'll have to look.

She stops, staring before her. TYRONE *sighs, shaking his head hopelessly, and attempts to catch his son's eye, looking for sympathy, but* EDMUND *is staring at the floor.*

TYRONE (*forces a casual tone*). Isn't it dinner time, dear? (*With a feeble attempt at teasing.*) You're for ever scolding me for being late, but now I'm on time for once, it's dinner that's late. (*She doesn't appear to hear him. He adds, still pleasantly.*) Well, if I can't eat yet, I can drink. I'd forgotten I had this.

He drinks his drink. EDMUND *watches him.* TYRONE *scowls and looks at his wife with sharp suspicion – roughly.*

Who's been tampering with my whiskey? The damned stuff is half water! Jamie's been away and he wouldn't overdo his trick like this, anyway. Any fool could tell – Mary, answer me! (*With angry disgust.*) I hope to God you haven't taken to drink on top of –

EDMUND. Shut up, Papa! (*To his mother, without looking at her.*) You treated Cathleen and Bridget, isn't that it, Mama?

MARY (*with indifferent casualness*). Yes, of course. They work hard for poor wages. And I'm the housekeeper, I have to keep them from leaving. Besides, I wanted to treat Cathleen because I had her drive uptown with me, and sent her to get my prescription filled.

EDMUND. For God's sake, Mama! You can't trust her! Do you want everyone on earth to know?

MARY (*her face hardening stubbornly*). Know what? That I suffer from rheumatism in my hands and have to take medicine to kill the pain? Why should I be ashamed of that? (*Turns on* EDMUND *with a hard, accusing antagonism – almost a revengeful enmity.*) I never knew what rheumatism was before you were born! Ask your father!

EDMUND *looks away, shrinking into himself.*

TYRONE. Don't mind her, lad. It doesn't mean anything. When she gets to the stage where she gives the old crazy excuse about her hands she's gone far away from us.

MARY (*turns on him – with a strangely triumphant, taunting smile*). I'm glad you realize that, James! Now perhaps you'll give up trying to remind me, you and Edmund! (*Abruptly, in a detached, matter-of-fact-tone.*) Why don't you light the light, James? It's getting dark. I know you hate to, but Edmund has proved to you that one bulb burning doesn't cost much. There's no sense letting your fear of the poorhouse make you too stingy.

TYRONE (*reacts mechanically*). I never claimed one bulb cost much! It's having them on, one here and one there, that makes the Electric Light Company rich. (*He gets up and turns on the reading lamp – roughly.*) But I'm a fool to talk reason to you. (*To* EDMUND.) I'll get a fresh bottle of whiskey, lad, and we'll have a real drink. (*He goes through the back parlour.*)

MARY (*with detached amusement*). He'll sneak around to the outside cellar door so the servants won't see him. He's really ashamed of keeping his whiskey padlocked in the cellar. Your father is a strange man, Edmund. It took many years before I understood him. You must try to understand and forgive him, too, and not feel contempt because he's close-fisted. His father deserted his mother and their six children a year or so after they came to America. He told them he had a premonition he would die soon, and he was homesick for Ireland, and wanted to go back there to die. So he went and he did die. He must have been a peculiar man, too. Your father had to go to work in a machine shop when he was only ten years old.

EDMUND (*protests dully*). Oh, for Pete's sake, Mama. I've heard Papa tell that machine-shop story ten thousand times.

MARY. Yes, dear, you've had to listen, but I don't think you've ever tried to understand.

EDMUND (*ignoring this – miserably*). Listen, Mama! You're not so far gone yet you've forgotten everything. You haven't asked me what I found out this afternoon. Don't you care a damn?

MARY (*shakenly*). Don't say that! You hurt me, dear!

EDMUND. What I've got is serious, Mama. Doc Hardy knows for sure now.

MARY (*stiffens into scornful, defensive stubbornness*). That lying old quack! I warned you he'd invent – !

EDMUND (*miserably dogged*). He called in a specialist to examine me, so he'd be absolutely sure.

MARY (*ignoring this*). Don't tell me about Hardy! If you heard what the doctor at the sanatorium, who really knows something, said about how he'd treated me! He said he ought to be locked up! He said it was a wonder I hadn't gone mad! I told him I had once, that time I ran down in my nightdress to throw myself off the dock. You remember that, don't you? And yet you want me to pay attention to what Doctor Hardy says. Oh, no!

EDMUND (*bitterly*). I remember, all right. It was right after that Papa and Jamie decided they couldn't hide it from me any more. Jamie told me. I called him a liar, I tried to punch him in the nose. But I knew he wasn't lying. (*His voice trembles, his eyes begin to fill with tears.*) God, it made everything in life seem rotten!

MARY (*pitiably*). Oh, don't. My baby! You hurt me so dreadfully!

EDMUND (*dully*). I'm sorry, Mama. It was you who brought it up. (*Then with a bitter, stubborn persistence.*) Listen, Mama. I'm going to tell you whether you want to hear or not. I've got to go to a sanatorium.

MARY (*dazedly, as if this was something that had never occurred to her*). Go away? (*Violently.*) No! I won't have it! How dare Doctor Hardy advise such a thing without consulting me! How dare your father allow him! What right has he? You are my baby! Let him attend to Jamie! (*More and more excited and bitter.*) I know why he wants you sent to a sanatorium. To take you from me! He's always tried to do that. He's been jealous of every one of my babies! He kept finding ways to make me leave them. That's what caused Eugene's death. He's been jealous of you most of all. He knew I loved you most because –

EDMUND (*miserably*). Oh, stop talking crazy, can't you, Mama! Stop trying to blame him. And why are you so against my going away now? I've been away a lot, and I've never noticed it broke your heart!

MARY (*bitterly*). I'm afraid you're not very sensitive, after all. (*Sadly.*) You might have guessed, dear, that after I knew you knew – about me – I had to be glad whenever you were where you couldn't see me.

EDMUND (*brokenly*). Mama! Don't! (*He reaches out blindly and takes her hand – but he drops it immediately, overcome by bitterness again.*) All this talk about loving me – and you won't even listen when I try to tell you how sick –

MARY (*with an abrupt transformation into a detached bullying motherliness*). Now, now. That's enough! I don't care to hear because I know it's nothing but Hardy's ignorant lies.

He shrinks back into himself. She keeps on in a forced, teasing tone but with an increasing undercurrent of resentment.

You're so like your father, dear. You love to make a scene out of nothing so you can be dramatic and tragic. (*With a belittling laugh.*) If I gave you the slightest encouragement, you'd tell me next you were going to die –

EDMUND. People do die of it. Your own father –

MARY (*sharply*). Why do you mention him? There's no comparison at all with you. He had consumption. (*Angrily.*) I hate you when you become gloomy and morbid! I forbid you to remind me of my father's death, do you hear me?

EDMUND (*his face hard – grimly*). Yes, I hear you, Mama. I wish to God I didn't. (*He gets up from his chair and stands staring condemningly at her – bitterly.*) It's pretty hard to take at times, having a dope fiend for a mother!

She winces – all life seeming to drain from her face, leaving it with the appearance of a plaster cast. Instantly EDMUND wishes he could take back what he has said. He stammers miserably.

Forgive me, Mama. I was angry. You hurt me.

There is a pause in which the foghorn and the ships' bells are heard.

MARY (*goes slowly to the windows at right like an automaton – looking out, a blank, far-off quality in her voice*). Just listen to that awful foghorn. And the bells. Why is it fog makes everything sound so sad and lost, I wonder?

EDMUND (*brokenly*). I – I can't stay here. I don't want any dinner.

He hurries away through the front parlour. She keeps staring out of the window until she hears the front door close behind him. Then she comes back and sits in her chair, the same blank look on her face.

MARY (*vaguely*). I must go upstairs. I haven't taken enough. (*She pauses – then longingly.*) I hope, sometime, without meaning it, I will take an overdose. I never could do it deliberately. The Blessed Virgin would never forgive me, then.

She hears TYRONE returning and turns as he comes in, through the back parlour, with a bottle of whiskey he has just uncorked. He is fuming.

TYRONE (*wrathfully*). The padlock is all scratched. That drunken loafer has tried to pick the lock with a piece of wire, the way he's done before. (*With satisfaction as if this was a perpetual battle of wits with his elder son.*) But I've fooled him this time. It's a special padlock a professional burglar couldn't pick. (*He puts the bottle on the tray and suddenly is aware of* EDMUND's *absence.*) Where's Edmund?

MARY (*with a vague far-away air*). He went out. Perhaps he's going uptown again to find Jamie. He still has some money left, I suppose, and it's burning a hole in his pocket. He said he didn't want any dinner. He doesn't seem to have any appetite these days. (*Then stubbornly.*) But it's just a summer cold.

TYRONE *stares at her and shakes his head helplessly and pours himself a big drink and drinks it. Suddenly it is too much for her and she breaks out and sobs.*

Oh, James, I'm so frightened! (*She gets up and throws her arms around him and hides her face on his shoulder – sobbingly.*) I know he's going to die!

TYRONE. Don't say that! It's not true! They promised me in six months he'd be cured.

MARY. You don't believe that! I can tell when you're acting! And it will be my fault. I should never have borne him. It would have been better for his sake. I could never hurt him then. He wouldn't have had to know his mother was a dope fiend – and hate her!

TYRONE (*his voice quivering*). Hush, Mary, for the love of God! He loves you. He knows it was a curse put on you without your knowing or willing it. He's proud you're his mother! (*Abruptly as he hears the pantry door opening.*) Hush, now! Here comes Cathleen. You don't want her to see you crying.

She turns quickly away from him to the windows at right, hastily wiping her eyes. A moment later CATHLEEN *appears in the back parlour doorway. She is uncertain in her walk and grinning woozily.*

CATHLEEN (*starts guiltily when she sees* TYRONE – *with dignity*). Dinner is served, Sir. (*Raising her voice unnecessarily.*) Dinner is served, Ma'am. (*She forgets her dignity and addresses* TYRONE *with good-natured familiarity.*) So you're here, are you? Well, well. Won't Bridget be in a rage! I told her the Madame said you wouldn't be home. (*Then reading accusation in his eye.*) Don't be looking at me that way. If I've taken a drop, I didn't steal it. I was invited. (*She turns with huffy dignity and disappears through the back parlour.*)

TYRONE (*sighs – then summoning his actor's heartiness*). Come along, dear. Let's have our dinner. I'm hungry as a hunter.

MARY (*comes to him – her face is composed in plaster again and her tone is remote*). I'm afraid you'll have to excuse me, James. I couldn't possibly eat anything. My hands pain me dreadfully. I think the best thing for me is to go to bed and rest. Good night, dear. (*She kisses him mechanically and turns toward the front parlour.*)

TYRONE (*harshly*). Up to take more of that God-damned poison, is that it? You'll be like a mad ghost before the night's over!

MARY (*starts to walk away – blankly*). I don't know what you're talking about, James. You say such mean, bitter things when you've drunk too much. You're as bad as Jamie or Edmund.

She moves off through the front parlour. He stands a second as if not knowing what to do. He is a sad, bewildered, broken old man. He walks wearily off through the back parlour toward the dining-room.

ACT FOUR

Scene. The same. It is around midnight. The lamp in the front hall has been turned out, so that now no light shines through the front parlour. In the living-room only the reading-lamp on the table is lighted. Outside the windows the wall of fog appears denser than ever. As the curtain rises, the foghorn is heard, followed by the ships' bells from the harbour.

TYRONE *is seated at the table. He wears his pince-nez, and is playing solitaire. He has taken off his coat and has on an old brown dressing-gown. The whiskey bottle on the tray is three-quarters empty. There is a fresh full bottle on the table, which he has brought from the cellar so there will be an ample reserve at hand. He is drunk and shows it by the owlish, deliberate manner in which he peers at each card to make certain of its identity, and then plays it as if he wasn't certain of his aim. His eyes have a misted, oily look and his mouth is slack. But despite all the whiskey in him, he has not escaped, and he looks as he appeared at the close of the preceding act, a sad, defeated old man, possessed by hopeless resignation.*

As the curtain rises, he finishes a game and sweeps the cards together. He shuffles them clumsily, dropping a couple on the floor. He retrieves them with difficulty, and starts to shuffle again, when he hears someone entering the front door. He peers over his pince-nez through the front parlour.

TYRONE (*his voice thick*). Who's that? Is it you, Edmund?

EDMUND's *voice answers curtly,* Yes. *Then he evidently collides with something in the dark hall and can be heard cursing. A moment later the hall lamp is turned on. TYRONE frowns and calls.*

Turn that light out before you come in.

But EDMUND *doesn't. He comes in through the front parlour. He is drunk now, too, but like his father he carries it well, and gives little physical sign of it except in his eyes and a chip-on-the-shoulder aggressiveness in his manner.* TYRONE *speaks, at first with a warm, relieved welcome.*

I'm glad you've come, lad. I've been damned lonely. (*Then resentfully.*) You're a fine one to run away and leave me to sit alone here all night when you know – (*With sharp irritation.*) I told you to turn out that light! We're not giving a ball. There's no reason to have the house ablaze with electricity at this time of night, burning up money!

EDMUND (*angrily*). Ablaze with electricity! One bulb! Hell, everyone keeps a light on in the front hall until they go to bed. (*He rubs his knee.*) I damned near busted my knee on the hat stand.

TYRONE. The light from here shows in the hall. You could see your way well enough if you were sober.

EDMUND. If *I* was sober? I like that!

TYRONE. I don't give a damn what other people do. If they want to be wasteful fools, for the sake of show, let them be!

EDMUND. One bulb! Christ, don't be such a cheap skate! I've proved by figures if you left the light bulb on all night it wouldn't be as much as one drink!

TYRONE. To hell with your figures! The proof is in the bills I have to pay!

EDMUND (*sits down opposite his father – contemptuously*). Yes, facts don't mean a thing, do they? What you want to believe, that's the only truth! (*Derisively.*) Shakespeare was an Irish Catholic, for example.

TYRONE (*stubbornly*). So he was. The proof is in his plays.

EDMUND. Well he wasn't, and there's no proof of it in his plays, except to you! (*Jeeringly.*) The Duke of Wellington, there was another good Irish Catholic!

TYRONE. I never said he was a good one. He was a renegade, but a Catholic just the same.

EDMUND. Well, he wasn't. You just want to believe no one but an Irish Catholic general could beat Napoleon.

TYRONE. I'm not going to argue with you. I asked you to turn out that light in the hall.

EDMUND. I heard you, and as far as I'm concerned it stays on.

TYRONE. None of your damned insolence! Are you going to obey me or not?

EDMUND. Not! If you want to be a crazy miser put it out yourself!

TYRONE (*with threatening anger*). Listen to me! I've put up with a lot from you because from the mad things you've done at times I've thought you weren't quite right in your head. I've excused you and never lifted my hand to you. But there's a straw that

breaks the camel's back. You'll obey me and put out that light
or, big as you are, I'll give you a thrashing that'll teach you – !
(*Suddenly he remembers* EDMUND's *illness and instantly becomes
guilty and shamefaced.*) Forgive me, lad. I forgot – You shouldn't
goad me into losing my temper.

EDMUND (*ashamed himself now*). Forget it, Papa. I apologize, too.
I had no right being nasty about nothing. I am a bit soused, I
guess. I'll put out the damned light. (*He starts to get up.*)

TYRONE. No, stay where you are. Let it burn. (*He stands up
abruptly – and a bit drunkenly – and begins turning on the three bulbs
in the chandelier, with a childish, bitterly dramatic self-pity.*) We'll
have them all on! Let them burn! To hell with them! The
poorhouse is the end of the road, and it might as well be
sooner as later! (*He finishes turning on the lights.*)

EDMUND (*has watched this proceeding with an awakened sense of
humour – now he grins, teasing affectionately*). That's a grand
curtain. (*He laughs.*) You're a wonder, Papa.

TYRONE (*sits down sheepishly – grumbles pathetically*). That's right, laugh
at the old fool! The poor old ham! But the final curtain will be in
the poorhouse just the same, and that's not comedy! (*Then as
EDMUND is still grinning, he changes the subject.*) Well, well, let's
not argue. You've got brains in that head of yours, though you
do your best to deny them. You'll live to learn the value of a
dollar. You're not like your damned tramp of a brother. I've
given up hope he'll ever get sense. Where is he, by the way?

EDMUND. How would I know?

TYRONE. I thought you'd gone back uptown to meet him.

EDMUND. No. I walked out to the beach. I haven't seen him
since this afternoon.

TYRONE. Well, if you split the money I gave you with him, like
a fool –

EDMUND. Sure I did. He's always staked me when he had
anything.

TYRONE. Then it doesn't take a soothsayer to tell he's probably
in the whorehouse.

EDMUND. What of it if he is? Why not?

TYRONE (*contemptuously*). Why not, indeed. It's the fit place for
him. If he's ever had a loftier dream than whores and whiskey,
he's never shown it.

EDMUND. Oh, for Pete's sake, Papa! If you're going to start that stuff, I'll beat it. (*He starts to get up.*)

TYRONE (*placatingly*). All right, all right, I'll stop. God knows, I don't like the subject either. Will you join me in a drink?

EDMUND. Ah! Now you're talking!

TYRONE (*passes the bottle to him – mechanically*). I'm wrong to treat you. You've had enough already.

EDMUND (*pouring a big drink – a bit drunkenly*). Enough is *not* as good as a feast. (*He hands back the bottle.*)

TYRONE. It's too much in your condition.

EDMUND. Forget my condition! (*He raises his glass.*) Here's how.

TYRONE. Drink hearty.

They drink.

If you walked all the way to the beach you must be damp and chilled.

EDMUND. Oh, I dropped in at the Inn on the way out and back.

TYRONE. It's not a night I'd pick for a long walk.

EDMUND. I loved the fog. It was what I needed. (*He sounds more tipsy and looks it.*)

TYRONE. You should have more sense than to risk –

EDMUND. To hell with sense! We're all crazy. What do we want with sense? (*He quotes from Dowson sardonically.*)

They are not long, the weeping and the laughter,
Love and desire and hate:
I think they have no portion in us after
We pass the gate.

They are not long, the days of wine and roses:
Out of a misty dream
Our path emerges for a while, then closes
Within a dream.

(*Staring before him.*) The fog was where I wanted to be. Halfway down the path you can't see this house. You'd never know it was here. Or any of the other places down the avenue. I couldn't see but a few feet ahead. I didn't meet a soul. Everything looked and sounded unreal. Nothing was what it is. That's what I wanted – to be alone with myself in another world where truth is untrue and life can hide from itself. Out beyond the harbour, where the road runs along the beach, I even lost the feeling of being on land. The fog and the sea seemed part of each other. It was like walking on the bottom of the sea. As if I had drowned long ago. As if I was a ghost belonging to the fog, and the fog was the ghost of the sea. It felt damned peaceful to be nothing more than a ghost within a ghost. (*He sees his father staring at him with mingled worry and irritated disapproval. He grins mockingly.*) Don't look at me as if I'd gone nutty. I'm talking sense. Who wants to see life as it is, if they can help it? It's the three Gorgons in one. You look in their faces and turn to stone. Or it's Pan. You see him and you die – that is, inside you – and have to go on living as a ghost.

TYRONE (*impressed and at the same time revolted*). You have a poet in you but it's a damned morbid one! (*Forcing a smile.*) Devil take your pessimism. I feel low-spirited enough. (*He sighs.*) Why can't you remember your Shakespeare and forget the third-raters? You'll find what you're trying to say in him – as you'll find everything else worth saying. (*He quotes, using his fine voice.*) 'We are such stuff as dreams are made on, and our little life is rounded with a sleep.'

EDMUND (*ironical*). Fine! That's beautiful. But I wasn't trying to say that. We are such stuff as manure is made on, so let's drink up and forget it. That's more my idea.

TYRONE (*disgustedly*). Ach! Keep such sentiments to yourself. I shouldn't have given you that drink.

EDMUND. It did pack a wallop, all right. On you, too. (*He grins with affectionate teasing.*) Even if you've never missed a performance! (*Aggressively.*) Well, what's wrong with being drunk? It's what we're after, isn't it? Let's not kid each other, Papa. Not tonight. We know what we're trying to forget. (*Hurriedly.*) But let's not talk about it. It's no use now.

TYRONE (*dully*). No. All we can do is try to be resigned – again.

EDMUND. Or be so drunk you can forget. (*He recites, and recites well, with bitter, ironical passion, the Symons' translation of Baudelaire's prose poem.*) 'Be always drunken. Nothing else matters: that is the only question. If you would not feel the horrible burden of Time weighing on your shoulders and crushing you to the earth, be drunken continually.

Drunken with what? With wine, with poetry, or with virtue as you will. But be drunken.

And if sometimes, on the stairs of a palace, or on the green
side of a ditch, or in the dreary solitude of your own room, you
should awaken and the drunkenness be half or wholly slipped
away from you, ask of the wind, or of the wave, or of the star,
or of the bird, or of the clock, of whatever flies, or sighs, or
rocks, or sings, or speaks, ask what hour it is; and the wind,
wave, star, bird, clock, will answer you: "It is the hour to be
drunken! Be drunken, if you would not be martyred slaves of
Time; be drunken continually! With wine, with poetry, or with
virtue, as you will."' (*He grins at his father provocatively.*)

TYRONE (*thickly humorous*). I wouldn't worry about the virtue
part of it, if I were you. (*Then disgustedly.*) Pah! It's morbid
nonsense! What little truth is in it you'll find nobly said in
Shakespeare. (*Then appreciatively.*) But you recited it well, lad.
Who wrote it?

EDMUND. Baudelaire.

TYRONE. Never heard of him.

EDMUND (*grins provocatively*). He also wrote a poem about Jamie
and the Great White Way –

TYRONE. That loafer! I hope to God he misses the last car and
has to stay uptown!

EDMUND (*goes on, ignoring this*). Although he was French and
never saw Broadway and died before Jamie was born. He knew
him and Little Old New York just the same. (*He recites the
Symons' translation of Baudelaire's 'Epilogue'.*

With heart at rest I climbed the citadel's
Steep height, and saw the city as from a tower,
Hospital, brothel, prison, and such hells,

Where evil comes up softly like a flower.
Thou knowest, O Satan, patron of my pain,
Not for vain tears I went up at that hour;

But like an old sad faithful lecher, fain
To drink delight of that enormous trull
Whose hellish beauty makes me young again.

Whether thou sleep, with heavy vapours full,
Sodden with day, or, new apparalled, stand
In gold-laced veils of evening beautiful,

I love thee, infamous city! Harlots and
Hunted have pleasures of their own to give,
The vulgar herd can never understand.

TYRONE (*with irritable disgust*). Morbid filth! Where the hell do you get your taste in literature? Filth and despair and pessimism! Another atheist, I suppose. When you deny God, you deny hope. That's the trouble with you. If you'd get down on your knees —

EDMUND (*as if he hadn't heard — sardonically*). It's a good likeness of Jamie, don't you think, hunted by himself and whiskey, hiding in a Broadway hotel room with some fat tart — he likes them fat — reciting Dowson's Cynara to her. (*He recites derisively, but with deep feeling.*)

All night upon mine heart I felt her warm heart beat,
Night long within mine arms in love and sleep she lay;
Surely the kisses of her bought red mouth were sweet;
But I was desolate and sick of an old passion,
When I awoke and found the dawn was gray:
I have been faithful to thee, Cynara! in my fashion.

(*Jeeringly.*) And the poor fat burlesque queen doesn't get a word of it, but suspects she's being insulted! And Jamie never loved any Cynara, and was never faithful to a woman in his life, even in his fashion! But he lies there, kidding himself he is superior and enjoys pleasures 'the vulgar herd can never understand'! (*He laughs.*) It's nuts — completely nuts!

TYRONE (*vaguely — his voice thick*). It's madness, yes. If you'd get on your knees and pray. When you deny God, you deny sanity.

EDMUND (*ignoring this*). But who am I to feel superior? I've done the same damned thing. And it's no more crazy than Dowson himself, inspired by an absinthe hangover, writing it to a dumb barmaid, who thought he was a poor crazy souse, and gave him the gate to marry a waiter! (*He laughs — then soberly, with genuine sympathy.*) Poor Dowson. Booze and consumption got him. (*He starts and for a second looks miserable and frightened. Then with defensive irony.*) Perhaps it would be tactful of me to change the subject.

TYRONE (*thickly*). Where you get your taste in authors — That damned library of yours! (*He indicates the small bookcase at rear.*) Voltaire, Rousseau, Schopenhauer, Nietzsche, Ibsen! Atheists, fools, and madmen! And your poets! This Dowson, and this Baudelaire, and Swinburne and Oscar Wilde, and Whitman and Poe! Whoremongers and degenerates! Pah! When I've three good sets of Shakespeare there (*he nods at the large bookcase*) you could read.

EDMUND (*provocatively*). They say he was a souse, too.

TYRONE. They lie! I don't doubt he liked his glass – it's a good man's failing – but he knew how to drink so it didn't poison his brain with morbidness and filth. Don't compare him wth the pack you've got in there. (*He indicates the small bookcase again.*) Your dirty Zola! And your Dante Gabriel Rossetti who was a dope fiend! (*He starts and looks guilty.*)

EDMUND (*with defensive dryness*). Perhaps it would be wise to change the subject. (*A pause.*) You can't accuse me of not knowing Shakespeare. Didn't I win five dollars from you once when you bet me I couldn't learn a leading part of his in a week, as you used to do in stock in the old days. I learned Macbeth and recited it letter-perfect, with you giving me the cues.

TYRONE (*approvingly*). That's true. So you did. (*He smiles teasingly and sighs.*) It was a terrible ordeal, I remember, hearing you murder the lines. I kept wishing I'd paid over the bet without making you prove it. (*He chuckles and* EDMUND *grins. Then he starts as he hears a sound from upstairs – with dread.*) Did you hear? She's moving around. I was hoping she'd gone to sleep.

EDMUND. Forget it! How about another drink? (*He reaches out and gets the bottle, pours a drink and hands it back. Then with a strained casualness, as his father pours a drink.*) When did Mama go to bed?

TYRONE. Right after you left. She wouldn't eat any dinner. What made you run away?

EDMUND. Nothing. (*Abruptly raising his glass.*) Well, here's how.

TYRONE (*mechanically*). Drink hearty, lad.

They drink. TYRONE *again listens to sounds upstairs – with dread.*

She's moving around a lot. I hope to God she doesn't come down.

EDMUND (*dully*). Yes. She'll be nothing but a ghost haunting the past by this time. (*He pauses – then miserably.*) Back before I was born –

TYRONE. Doesn't she do the same with me? Back before she ever knew me. You'd think the only happy days she's ever known were in her father's home, or at the Convent, praying and playing the piano. (*Jealous resentment in his bitterness.*) As I've told you before, you must take her memories with a grain of salt. Her wonderful home was ordinary enough. Her father wasn't the great, generous, noble Irish gentleman she makes out. He was a nice enough man, good company and a good talker. I liked him and he liked me. He was prosperous enough, too, in his wholesale grocery business, an able man. But he had his weakness. She condemns my drinking but she forgets his. It's true he never touched a drop till he was forty, but after that he made up for lost time. He became a steady champagne drinker, the worst kind. That was his grand pose, to drink only champagne. Well, it finished him quick – that and the consumption – (*He stops with a guilty glance at his son.*)

EDMUND (*sardonically*). We don't seem able to avoid unpleasant topics, do we?

TYRONE (*sighs sadly*). No. (*Then with a pathetic attempt at heartiness.*) What do you say to a game or two of Casino, lad?

EDMUND. All right.

TYRONE (*shuffling the cards clumsily*). We can't lock up and go to bed till Jamie comes on the last trolley – which I hope he won't – and I don't want to go upstairs, anyway, till she's asleep.

EDMUND. Neither do I.

TYRONE (*keeps shuffling the cards fumblingly, forgetting to deal them*). As I was saying, you must take her tales of the past with a grain of salt. The piano playing and her dream of becoming a concert pianist. That was put in her head by the nuns flattering her. She was their pet. They loved her for being so devout. They're innocent women, anyway, when it comes to the world. They don't know that not one in a million who shows promise ever rises to concert playing. Not that your mother didn't play well for a schoolgirl, but that's no reason to take it for granted she could have –

EDMUND (*sharply*). Why don't you deal, if we're going to play.

TYRONE. Eh? I am. (*Dealing with very uncertain judgement of distance.*) And the idea she might have become a nun. That's the worst. Your mother was one of the most beautiful girls you could ever see. She knew it, too. She was a bit of a rogue and a coquette, God bless her, behind all her shyness and blushes. She was never made to renounce the world. She was bursting with health and high spirits and the love of loving.

EDMUND. For God's sake, Papa! Why don't you pick up your hand?

TYRONE (*picks it up – dully*). Yes, let's see what I have here.

They both stare at their cards unseeingly. Then they both start.
TYRONE *whispers.*

Listen!

EDMUND. She's coming downstairs.

TYRONE (*hurriedly*). We'll play our game. Pretend not to notice and she'll soon go up again.

EDMUND (*staring through the front parlour – with relief*). I don't see her. She must have started down and then turned back.

TYRONE. Thank God.

EDMUND. Yes. It's pretty horrible to see her the way she must be now. (*With bitter misery.*) The hardest thing to take is the blank wall she builds around her. Or it's more like a bank of fog in which she hides and loses herself. Deliberately, that's the hell of it! You know something in her does it deliberately – to get beyond our reach, to be rid of us, to forget we're alive! It's as if, in spite of loving us, she hated us!

TYRONE (*remonstrates gently*). Now, now, lad. It's not her. It's the damned poison.

EDMUND (*bitterly*). She takes it to get that effect. At least, I know she did this time! (*Abruptly.*) My play, isn't it? Here. (*He plays a card.*)

TYRONE (*plays mechanically – gently reproachful*). She's been terribly frightened about your illness, for all her pretending. Don't be too hard on her, lad. Remember she's not responsible. Once that cursed poison gets a hold on anyone –

EDMUND (*his face grows hard and he stares at his father with bitter accusation*). It never should have gotten a hold on her! I know damned well she's not to blame! And I know who is! You are! Your damned stinginess! If you'd spent money for a decent doctor when she was so sick after I was born, she'd never have known morphine existed! Instead you put her in the hands of a hotel quack who wouldn't admit his ignorance and took the easiest way out, not giving a damn what happened to her afterwards! All because his fee was cheap! Another one of your bargains!

TYRONE (*stung – angrily*). Be quiet! How dare you talk of something you know nothing about! (*Trying to control his temper.*)

You must try to see my side of it, too, lad. How was I to know he was that kind of a doctor? He had a good reputation –

EDMUND. Among the souses in the hotel bar, I suppose!

TYRONE. That's a lie! I asked the hotel proprietor to recommend the best –

EDMUND. Yes! At the same time crying poorhouse and making it plain you wanted a cheap one! I know your system! By God, I ought to after this afternoon!

TYRONE (*guiltily defensive*). What about this afternoon?

EDMUND. Never mind now. We're talking about Mama! I'm saying no matter how you excuse yourself you know damned well your stinginess is to blame –

TYRONE. And I say you're a liar! Shut your mouth right now, or –

EDMUND (*ignoring this*). After you found out she'd been made a morphine addict, why didn't you send her to a cure then, at the start, while she still had a chance? No, that would have meant spending some money! I'll bet you told her all she had to do was use a little will-power! That's what you still believe in your heart, in spite of what doctors, who really know something about it, have told you!

TYRONE. You lie again! I know better than that now! But how was I to know then? What did I know of morphine? It was three years before I discovered what was wrong. I thought she'd never got over her sickness, that's all. Why didn't I send her to a cure, you say? (*Bitterly.*) Haven't I? I've spent thousands upon thousands in cures! A waste. What good have they done her? She always started again.

EDMUND. Because you've never given her anything that would help her want to stay off it! No home except this summer dump in a place she hates and you've refused even to spend money to make this look decent, while you keep buying more property, and playing sucker for every con man with a gold mine, or a silver mine, or any kind of get-rich-quick swindle! You've dragged her around on the road, season after season, on one-night stands, with no one she could talk to, waiting night after night in dirty hotel rooms for you to come back with a bun on after the bars closed! Christ, is it any wonder she didn't want to be cured. Jesus, when I think of it I hate your guts!

TYRONE (*strickenly*). Edmund! (*Then in a rage.*) How dare you talk to your father like that, you insolent young cub! After all I've done for you.

EDMUND. We'll come to that, what you're doing for me!

TYRONE (*looking guilty again – ignores this*). Will you stop repeating your mother's crazy accusations, which she never makes unless it's the poison talking? I never dragged her on the road against her will. Naturally, I wanted her with me. I loved her. And she came because she loved me and wanted to be with me. That's the truth, no matter what she says when she's not herself. And she needn't have been lonely. There was always the members of my company to talk to, if she'd wanted to. She had her children, too, and I insisted, in spite of the expense, on having a nurse to travel with her.

EDMUND (*bitterly*). Yes, your one generosity, and that because you were jealous of her paying too much attention to us, and wanted us out of your way! It was another mistake, too! If she'd had to take care of me all by herself, and had that to occupy her mind, maybe she'd have been able –

TYRONE (*goaded into vindictiveness*). Or for that matter, if you insist on judging things by what she says when she's not in her right mind, if you hadn't been born she'd never – (*He stops ashamed.*)

EDMUND (*suddenly spent and miserably*). Sure. I know that's what she feels, Papa.

TYRONE (*protests penitently*). She doesn't! She loves you as dearly as ever mother loved a son! I only said that because you put me in such a God-damned rage, raking up the past, and saying you hate me –

EDMUND (*dully*). I didn't mean it, Papa. (*He suddenly smiles – kidding a bit drunkenly.*) I'm like Mama, I can't help liking you, in spite of everything.

TYRONE (*grins a bit drunkenly in return*). I might say the same of you. You're no great shakes as a son. It's a case of 'A poor thing but mine own.'

They both chuckle with real, if alcoholic, affection. TYRONE *changes the subject.*

What's happened to our game? Whose play is it?

EDMUND. Yours, I guess.

TYRONE *plays a card which* EDMUND *takes and the game gets forgotten again.*

TYRONE. You mustn't let yourself be too downhearted, lad, by the news you had today. Both the doctors promised me, if you obey orders at this place you're going, you'll be cured in six months, or a year at most.

EDMUND (*his face hard again*). Don't kid me. You don't believe that.

TYRONE (*too vehemently*). Of course I believe it! Why shouldn't I believe it when both Hardy and the specialist – ?

EDMUND. You think I'm going to die.

TYRONE. That's a lie! You're crazy!

EDMUND (*more bitterly*). So why waste money? That's why you're sending me to a state farm –

TYRONE (*in guilty confusion*). What state farm? It's the Hilltown Sanatorium, that's all I know, and both doctors said it was the best place for you.

EDMUND (*scathingly*). For the money! That is, for nothing, or practically nothing. Don't lie, Papa! You know damned well Hilltown Sanatorium is a state institution! Jamie suspected you'd cry poorhouse to Hardy and he wormed the truth out of him.

TYRONE (*furiously*). That drunken loafer! I'll kick him out in the gutter! He's poisoned your mind against me ever since you were old enough to listen!

EDMUND. You can't deny it's the truth about the state farm, can you?

TYRONE. It's not true the way you look at it! What if it is run by the state? That's nothing against it. The state has the money to make a better place than any private sanatorium. And why shouldn't I take advantage of it? It's my right – and yours. We're residents. I'm a property owner. I help to support it. I'm taxed to death –

EDMUND (*with bitter irony*). Yes, on property valued at a quarter of a million.

TYRONE. Lies! It's all mortgaged!

EDMUND. Hardy and the specialist know what you're worth. I wonder what they thought of you when they heard you moaning poorhouse and showing you wanted to wish me on charity!

TYRONE. It's a lie! All I told them was I couldn't afford any millionaire's sanatorium because I was land poor. That's the truth!

EDMUND. And then you went to the Club to meet McGuire and let him stick you with another bum piece of property! (*As* TYRONE *starts to deny.*) Don't lie about it! We met McGuire in the hotel bar after he left you. Jamie kidded him about hooking you, and he winked and laughed!

TYRONE (*lying feebly*). He's a liar if he said –

EDMUND. Don't lie about it! (*With gathering intensity.*) God, Papa, ever since I went to sea and was on my own, and found out what hard work for little pay was, and what it felt like to be broke, and starve, and camp on park benches because I had no place to sleep, I've tried to be fair to you because I knew what you'd been up against as a kid. I've tried to make allowances. Christ, you have to make allowances in this damned family or go nuts! I have tried to make allowances for myself when I remember all the rotten stuff I've pulled! I've tried to feel like Mama that you can't help being what you are where money is concerned. But God Almighty, this last stunt of yours is too much! It makes me want to puke! Not because of the rotten way you're treating me. To hell with that! I've treated you rottenly, in my way, more than once. But to think when it's a question of your son having consumption, you can show yourself up before the whole town as a stinking old tightwad! Don't you know Hardy will talk and the whole damned town will know? Jesus, Papa, haven't you any pride or shame? (*Bursting with rage.*) And don't think I'll let you get away with it! I won't go to any damned state farm just to save you a few lousy dollars to buy more bum property with! You stinking old miser – ! (*He chokes huskily, his voice trembling with rage, and then is shaken by a fit of coughing.*)

TYRONE (*has shunk back in his chair under this attack, his guilty contrition greater than his anger. He stammers*). Be quiet! Don't say that to me! You're drunk! I won't mind you. Stop coughing, lad. You've got yourself worked up over nothing. Who said you had to go to this Hilltown place? You can go anywhere you like. I don't give a damn what it costs. All I care about is to have you get well. Don't call me a stinking miser, just because I don't want doctors to think I'm a millionaire they can swindle.

EDMUND *has stopped coughing. He looks sick and weak. His father stares at him frightenedly.*

You look weak, lad. You'd better take a bracer.

EDMUND (*grabs the bottle and pours his glass brimful – weakly*). Thanks. (*He gulps down the whiskey.*)

TYRONE (*pours himself a big drink, which empties the bottle, and drinks it. His head bows and he stares dully at the cards on the table – vaguely*). Whose play is it? (*He goes on dully, without resentment.*) A stinking old miser. Well, maybe you're right. Maybe I can't help being, although all my life since I had anything I've thrown money over the bar to buy drinks for everyone in the house, or loaned money to spongers I knew would never pay it back –(*With a loose-mouthed sneer of self-contempt.*) But, of course, that was in bar-rooms, when I was full of whiskey. I can't feel that way about it when I'm sober in my home. It was at home I first learned the value of a dollar and the fear of the poorhouse. I've never been able to believe in my luck since. I've always feared it would change and everything I had would be taken away. But still, the more property you own, the safer you think you are. That may not be logical, but it's the way I have to feel. Banks fail, and your money's gone, but you think you can keep land beneath your feet. (*Abruptly his tone becomes scornfully superior.*) You said you realized what I'd been up against as a boy. The hell you do! How could you? You've had everything – nurses, schools, college, though you didn't stay there. You've had food, clothing. Oh, I know you had a fling of hard work with your back and hands, a bit of being homeless and penniless in a foreign land, and I respect you for it. But it was a game of romance and adventure to you. It was play.

EDMUND (*dully sarcastic*). Yes, particularly the time I tried to commit suicide at Jimmie the Priest's, and almost did.

TYRONE. You weren't in your right mind. No son of mine would ever – You were drunk.

EDMUND. I was stone cold sober. That was the trouble. I'd stopped to think too long.

TYRONE (*with drunken peevishness*). Don't start your damned atheist morbidness again! I don't care to listen. I was trying to make plain to you – (*Scornfully.*) What do you know of the value of a dollar? When I was ten my father deserted my mother and went back to Ireland to die. Which he did soon enough, and deserved to, and I hope he's roasting in hell. He mistook rat poison for flour, or sugar, or something. There was gossip it wasn't by mistake but that's a lie. No one in my family ever –

EDMUND. My bet is, it wasn't by mistake.

TYRONE. More morbidness! Your brother put that in your head. The worst he can suspect is the only truth for him. But never mind. My mother was left, a stranger in a strange land, with four small children, me and a sister a little older and two younger than me. My two older brothers had moved to other parts. They couldn't help. They were hard put to it to keep themselves alive. There was no damned romance in our poverty. Twice we were evicted from the miserable hovel we called home, with my mother's few sticks of furniture thrown out in the street, and my mother and sisters crying. I cried, too, though I tried hard not to, because I was the man of the family. At ten years old! There was no more school for me. I worked twelve hours a day in a machine shop, learning to make files. A dirty barn of a place where rain dripped through the roof, where you roasted in summer, and there was no stove in winter, and your hands got numb with cold, where the only light came through two small filthy windows, so on grey days I'd have to sit bent over with my eyes almost touching the files in order to see! You talk of work! And what do you think I got for it! Fifty cents a week! It's the truth! Fifty cents a week! And my poor mother washed and scrubbed for the Yanks by the day, and my older sister sewed, and my two younger stayed at home to keep the house. We never had clothes enough to wear, nor enough food to eat. Well I remember one Thanksgiving, or maybe it was Christmas, when some Yank in whose house mother had been scrubbing gave her a dollar extra for a present, and on the way home she spent it all on food. I can remember her hugging and kissing us and saying with tears of joy running down her tired face: 'Glory be to God, for once in our lives we'll have enough for each of us!' (*He wipes tears from his eyes.*) A fine, brave, sweet woman. There never was a braver or finer.

EDMUND (*moved*). Yes, she must have been.

TYRONE. Her one fear was she'd get old and sick and have to die in the poorhouse. (*He pauses – then adds with grim humour.*) It was in those days I learned to be a miser. A dollar was worth so much then. And once you've learned a lesson, it's hard to unlearn it. You have to look for bargains. If I took this state farm sanatorium for a good bargain, you'll have to forgive me. The doctors did tell me it's a good place. You must believe that, Edmund. And I swear I never meant you to go there if you didn't want to. (*Vehemently.*) You can choose any place you like! Never mind what it costs! Any place I can afford. Any place you like – within reason.

At this qualification, a grin twitches EDMUND's *lips. His resentment has gone. His father goes on with an elaborately offhand, casual air.*

There was another sanatorium the specialist recommended. He said it had a record as good as any place in the country. It's endowed by a group of millionaire factory owners, for the benefit of their workers principally, but you're eligible to go there because you're a resident. There's such a pile of money behind it, they don't have to charge much. It's only seven dollars a week but you get ten times that value. (*Hastily.*) I don't want to persuade you to anything, understand. I'm simply repeating what I was told.

EDMUND (*concealing his smile – casually*). Oh, I know that. It sounds like a good bargain to me. I'd like to go there. So that settles that. (*Abruptly he is miserably desperate again – dully.*) It doesn't matter a damn now, anyway. Let's forget it! (*Changing the subject.*) How about our game? Whose play is it?

TYRONE (*mechanically*). I don't know. Mine, I guess. No, it's yours.

EDMUND *plays a card. His father takes it. Then about to play from his hand, he again forgets the game.*

Yes, maybe life overdid the lesson for me, and made a dollar worth too much, and the time came when that mistake ruined my career as a fine actor. (*Sadly.*) I've never admitted this to anyone before, lad, but tonight I'm so heartsick I feel at the end of everything, and what's the use of fake pride and pretence. That God-damned play I bought for a song and made such a great success in – a great money success – it ruined me with its promise of an easy fortune. I didn't want to do anything else, and by the time I woke up to the fact I'd become a slave to the damned thing and did try other plays, it was too late. They had identified me with that one part, and didn't want me in anything else. They were right, too. I'd lost the great talent I once had through years of easy repetition, never learning a new part, never really working hard. Thirty-five to forty thousand dollars net profit a season like snapping

your fingers! It was too great a temptation. Yet before I bought
the damned thing I was considered one of the three or four
young actors with the greatest artistic promise in America. I'd
worked like hell. I'd left a good job as a machinist to take
supers' parts because I loved the theatre. I was wild with
ambition. I read all the plays ever written. I studied
Shakespeare as you'd study the Bible. I educated myself. I got
rid of an Irish brogue you could cut with a knife. I loved
Shakespeare. I would have acted in any of his plays for
nothing, for the joy of being alive in his great poetry. And I
acted well in him. I felt inspired by him. I could have been a
great Shakespearean actor, if I'd kept on. I know that! In 1874
when Edwin Booth came to the theatre in Chicago where I was
leading man, I played Cassius to his Brutus one night, Brutus
to his Cassius the next, Othello to his Iago, and so on. The first
night I played Othello, he said to our manager, 'That young
man is playing Othello better than I ever did!' (*Proudly.*) That
from Booth, the greatest actor of his day or any other! And it
was true! And I was only twenty-seven years old! As I look back
on it now, that night was the high spot in my career. I had life
where I wanted it! And for a time after that I kept on upward
with ambition high. Married your mother. Ask her what I was
like in those days. Her love was an added incentive to ambition.
But a few years later my good bad luck made me find the big
money-maker. It wasn't that in my eyes at first. It was a great
romantic part I knew I could play better than anyone. But it
was a great box-office success from the start – and then life had
me where it wanted me – at from thirty-five to forty thousand
net profit a season! A fortune in those days – or even in these.
(*Bitterly.*) What the hell was it I wanted to buy, I wonder, that
was worth – Well, no matter. It's a late day for regrets. (*He
glances vaguely at his cards.*) My play, isn't it?

EDMUND (*moved, stares at his father with understanding – slowly*).
I'm glad you've told me this, Papa. I know you a lot better now.

TYRONE (*with a loose, twisted smile*). Maybe I shouldn't have told
you. Maybe you'll only feel more contempt for me. And it's a
poor way to convince you of the value of a dollar. (*Then as if
this phrase automatically aroused an habitual association in his mind,
he glances up at the chandelier disapprovingly.*) The glare from
those extra lights hurts my eyes. You don't mind if I turn them
out, do you? We don't need them, and there's no use making
the Electric Company rich.

EDMUND (*controlling a wild impulse to laugh – agreeably*). No, sure not. Turn them out.

TYRONE (*gets heavily and a bit waveringly to his feet and gropes uncertainly for the lights – his mind going back to its line of thought*). No, I don't know what the hell it was I wanted to buy. (*He clicks out one bulb.*) On my solemn oath, Edmund, I'd gladly face not having an acre of land to call my own, nor a penny in the bank – (*He clicks out another bulb.*) I'd be willing to have no home but the poorhouse in my old age if I could look back now on having been the fine artist I might have been.

He turns out the third bulb, so only the reading lamp is on, and sits down again heavily. EDMUND suddenly cannot hold back a burst of strained, ironical laughter. TYRONE is hurt.

What the devil are you laughing at?

EDMUND. Not at you, Papa. At life. It's so damned crazy.

TYRONE (*growls*). More of your morbidness! There's nothing wrong with life. It's we who – (*He quotes.*) 'The fault, dear Brutus, is not in our stars, but in ourselves that we are underlings.' (*He pauses – then sadly.*) The praise Edwin Booth gave my Othello. I made the manager put down his exact words in writing. I kept it in my wallet for years. I used to read it every once in a while until finally it made me feel so bad I didn't want to face it any more. Where is it now, I wonder? Somewhere in this house. I remember I put it away carefully –

EDMUND (*with a wry ironical sadness*). It might be in an old trunk in the attic, along with Mama's wedding dress. (*Then as his father stares at him, he adds quickly.*) For Pete's sake, if we're going to play cards, let's play.

He takes the card his father has played and leads. For a moment, they play the game, like mechanical chess players. Then TYRONE stops, listening to a sound upstairs.

TYRONE. She's still moving around. God knows when she'll go to sleep.

EDMUND (*pleads tensely*). For Christ's sake, Papa, forget it!

He reaches out and pours a drink. TYRONE starts to protest, then gives it up. EDMUND drinks. He puts down the glass. His expression changes. When he speaks it is as if he were deliberately giving way to drunkenness and seeking to hide behind a maudlin manner.

Yes, she moves above and beyond us, a ghost haunting the past, and here we sit pretending to forget, but straining our ears listening for the slightest sound, hearing the fog drip from the eaves like the uneven tick of a rundown, crazy clock – or like the dreary tears of a trollop spattering in a puddle of stale beer on a honky-tonk table top! (*He laughs with maudlin appreciation.*) Not so bad, that last, eh? Original, not Baudelaire. Give me credit! (*Then with alcoholic talkativeness.*) You've just told me some high spots in your memories. Want to hear mine? They're all connected with the sea. Here's one. When I was on the Squarehead square rigger, bound for Buenos Aires. Full moon in the Trades. The old hooker driving fourteen knots. I lay on the bowsprit, facing astern, with the water foaming into spume under me, the masts with every sail white in the moonlight, towering high above me. I became drunk with the beauty and singing rhythm of it, and for a moment I lost myself – actually lost my life. I was set free! I dissolved in the sea, became white sails and flying spray, became beauty and rhythm, became moonlight and the ship and the high dim-starred sky! I belonged, without past or future, within peace and unity and a wild joy, within something greater than my own life, or the life of Man, to Life itself! To God, if you want to put it that way. Then another time, on the American Line, when I was lookout on the crow's nest in the dawn watch. A calm sea, that time. Only a lazy ground swell and a slow drowsy roll of the ship. The passengers asleep and none of the crew in sight. No sound of man. Black smoke pouring from the funnels behind and beneath me. Dreaming, not keeping lookout, feeling alone, and above, and apart, watching the dawn creep like a painted dream over the sky and sea which slept together. Then the moment of ecstatic freedom came. The peace, the end of the quest, the last harbour, the joy of belonging to a fulfilment beyond men's lousy, pitiful, greedy fears and hopes and dreams! And several other times in my life, when I was swimming far out, or lying alone on a beach, I have had the same experience. Became the sun, the hot sand, green seaweed anchored to a rock, swaying in the tide. Like a saint's vision of beatitude. Like the veil of things as they seem drawn back by an unseen hand. For a second you see – and seeing the secret, are the secret. For a second there is meaning! Then the hand lets the veil fall and you are alone, lost in the fog again, and you stumble on toward nowhere, for no good reason! (*He grins wryly.*) It was a great mistake, my being born a man, I would have been much more successful as a sea-gull or a fish. As it is,

I will always be a stranger who never feels at home, who does not really want and is not really wanted, who can never belong, who must always be a little in love with death!

TYRONE (*stares at him – impressed*). Yes, there's the making of a poet in you all right. (*Then protesting uneasily.*) But that's morbid craziness about not being wanted and loving death.

EDMUND (*sardonically*). The *makings* of a poet. No, I'm afraid I'm like the guy who is always panhandling for a smoke. He hasn't even got the makings. He's got only the habit. I couldn't touch what I tried to tell you just now. I just stammered. That's the best I'll ever do. I mean, if I live. Well, it will be faithful realism, at least. Stammering is the native eloquence of us fog people.

A pause. Then they both jump startledly as there is a noise from outside the house, as if someone had stumbled and fallen on the front steps. EDMUND *grins.*

Well, that sounds like the absent brother. He must have a peach of a bun on.

TYRONE (*scowling*). That loafer! He caught the last car, bad luck to it. (*He gets to his feet.*) Get him to bed, Edmund. I'll go out on the porch. He has a tongue like an adder when he's drunk. I'd only lose my temper.

He goes out of the door to the side porch as the front door in the hall bangs shut behind JAMIE. EDMUND *watches with amusement* JAMIE's *wavering progress through the front parlour.* JAMIE *comes in. He is very drunk and woozy on his legs. His eyes are glassy, his face bloated, his speech blurred, his mouth slack like his father's, a leer on his lips.*

JAMIE (*swaying and blinking in the doorway – in a loud voice*). What ho! What ho!

EDMUND (*sharply*). Nix on the loud noise!

JAMIE (*blinks at him*). Oh, hello, Kid. (*With great seriousness.*) I'm as drunk as a fiddler's bitch.

EDMUND (*dryly*). Thanks for telling me your great secret.

JAMIE (*grins foolishly*). Yes. Unnecessary information Number One, eh? (*He bends and slaps at the knees of his trousers.*) Had serious accident. The fron' steps tried to trample on me. Took advantage of fog to waylay me. Ought to be a lighthouse out there. Dark in here, too. (*Scowling.*) What the hell is this, the morgue? Lesh have some light on sibject. (*He sways forward to the table, reciting Kipling.*)

Ford, ford, ford, o' Kabul river,
Ford o' Kabul river in the dark!
Keep the crossing-stakes beside you, an' they will surely guide you
'Cross the ford o' Kabul river in the dark.

(*He fumbles at the chandelier and manages to turn on the three bulbs.*)

Thash more like it. To hell with old Gaspard. Where is the old tightwad?

EDMUND. Out on the porch.

JAMIE. Can't expect us to live in the Black Hole of Calcutta. (*His eyes fix on the full bottle of whiskey.*) Say! Have I got the d.t.'s? (*He reaches out fumblingly and grabs it.*) By God, it's real. What's matter with the Old Man tonight? Must be ossified to forget he left this out. Grab opportunity by the forelock. Key to my success. (*He slops a big drink into a glass.*)

EDMUND. You're stinking now. That will knock you stiff.

JAMIE. Wisdom from the mouth of babes. Can the wise stuff, Kid. You're still wet behind the ears. (*He lowers himself into a chair, holding the drink carefully aloft.*)

EDMUND. All right. Pass out if you want to.

JAMIE. Can't, that's trouble. Had enough to sink a ship, but can't sink. Well, here's hoping. (*He drinks.*)

EDMUND. Shove over the bottle. I'll have one, too.

JAMIE (*with sudden, big-brotherly solicitude, grabbing the bottle*). No, you don't. Not while I'm around. Remember doctor's orders. Maybe no one else gives a damn if you die, but I do. My kid brother. I love your guts, Kid. Everything else is gone. You're all I've got left. (*Pulling bottle closer to him.*) So no booze for you, if I can help it. (*Beneath his drunken sentimentality there is a genuine sincerity.*)

EDMUND (*irritably*). Oh, lay off it.

JAMIE (*is hurt and his face hardens*). You don't believe I care, eh? Just drunken bull. (*He shoves the bottle over.*) All right. Go ahead and kill yourself.

EDMUND (*seeing he is hurt – affectionately*). Sure I know you care, Jamie, and I'm going on the wagon. But tonight doesn't count.

Too many damned things have happened today. (*He pours a drink.*) Here's how. (*He drinks.*)

JAMIE (*sobers up momentarily and with a pitying look*). I know, Kid. It's been a lousy day for you. (*Then with sneering cynicism.*) I'll bet old Gaspard hasn't tried to keep you off booze. Probably gave you the case to take with you to the state farm for pauper patients. The sooner you kick the bucket, the less expense. (*With contemptuous hatred.*) What a bastard to have for a father! Christ, if you put him in a book, no one would believe it!

EDMUND (*defensively*). Oh, Papa's all right, if you try to understand him – and keep your sense of humour.

JAMIE (*cynically*). He's been putting on the old sob act for you, eh? He can always kid you. But not me. Never again. (*Then slowly.*) Although, in a way, I do feel sorry for him about one thing. But he has even that coming to him. He's to blame. (*Hurriedly.*) But to hell with that. (*He grabs the bottle and pours another drink, appearing very drunk again.*) That lash drink's getting me. This one ought to put the lights out. Did you tell Gaspard I got it out of Doc Hardy this sanatorium is a charity dump?

EDMUND (*reluctantly*). Yes. I told him I wouldn't go there. It's all settled now. He said I can go anywhere I want. (*He adds, smiling without resentment.*) Within reason, of course.

JAMIE (*drunkenly imitating his father*). Of course, lad. Anything within reason. (*Sneering.*) That means another cheap dump. Old Gaspard, the miser in 'The Bells', that's a part he can play without make-up.

EDMUND (*irritably*). Oh, shut up, will you. I've heard that Gaspard stuff a million times.

JAMIE (*shrugs his shoulders – thickly*). Aw right, if you're shatisfied – let him get away with it. It's your funeral – I mean, I hope it won't be.

EDMUND (*changing the subject*). What did you do uptown tonight? Go to Mamie Burns?

JAMIE (*very drunk, his head nodding*). Sure thing. Where else could I find suitable feminine companionship? And love. Don't forget love. What is a man without a good woman's love? A God-damned hollow shell.

EDMUND (*chuckles tipsily, letting himself go now and be drunk*). You're a nut.

JAMIE (*quotes with gusto from Oscar Wilde's 'The Harlot's House'.*)

Then, turning to my love, I said,
'The dead are dancing with the dead,
'The dust is whirling with the dust.'

But she – she heard the violin,
And left my side and entered in:
Love passed into the house of lust.

Then suddenly the tune went false,
The dancers wearied of the waltz . . .

(*He breaks off, thickly.*) Not strictly accurate. If my love was with me, I didn't notice it. She must have been a ghost. (*He pauses.*) Guess which one of Mamie's charmers I picked to bless me with her woman's love. It'll hand you a laugh, Kid. I picked Fat Violet.

EDMUND (*laughs drunkenly*). No, honest? Some pick! God, she weighs a ton. What the hell for, a joke?

JAMIE. No joke. Very serious. By the time I hit Mamie's dump I felt very sad about myself and all the other poor bums in the world. Ready for a weep on any old womanly bosom. You know how you get when John Barleycorn turns on the soft music inside you. Then, soon as I got in the door, Mamie began telling me all her troubles. Beefed how rotten business was, and she was going to give Fat Violet the gate. Customers didn't fall for Vi. Only reason she'd kept her was she could play the piano. Lately Vi's gone on drunks and been too boiled to play, and was eating her out of house and home, and although Vi was a goodhearted dumbbell, and she felt sorry for her because she didn't know how the hell she'd make a living, still business was business, and she couldn't afford to run a home for fat tarts. Well, that made me feel sorry for Fat Violet, so I squandered two bucks of your dough to escort her upstairs. With no dishonourable intentions whatever. I like them fat, but not that fat. All I wanted was a little heart-to-heart talk concerning the infinite sorrow of life.

EDMUND (*chuckles drunkenly*). Poor Vi! I'll bet you recited Kipling and Swinburne and Dowson and gave her 'I have been faithful to thee, Cynara, in my fashion.'

JAMIE (*grins loosely*). Sure – with the Old Master, John Barleycorn, playing soft music. She stood it for a while. Then she got good and sore. Got the idea I took her upstairs for a

joke. Gave me a grand bawling out. Said she was better than a
drunken bum who recited poetry. Then she began to cry. So I
had to say I loved her because she was fat, and she wanted to
believe that, and I stayed with her to prove it, and that cheered
her up, and she kissed me when I left, and said she'd fallen
hard for me, and we both cried a little more in the hallway,
and everything was fine, except Mamie Burns thought I'd gone
bughouse.

EDMUND (*quotes derisively*).

Harlots and
Hunted have pleasures of their own to give,
The vulgar herd can never understand.

JAMIE (*nods his head drunkenly*). Egzactly! Hell of a good time, at
that. You should have stuck around with me, Kid. Mamie
Burns inquired after you. Sorry to hear you were sick. She
meant it, too. (*He pauses – then with a maudlin humour, in a ham-
actor tone.*) This night has opened my eyes to a great career in
store for me, my boy! I shall give the art of acting back to the
performing seals, which are its most perfect expression. By
applying my natural God-given talents in their proper sphere, I
shall attain the pinnacle of success! I'll be the lover of the fat
woman in Barnum and Bailey's circus!

EDMUND *laughs*. JAMIE*'s mood changes to arrogant disdain.*

Pah! Imagine me sunk to the fat girl in a hick town hooker
shop! Me! Who have made some of the best-lookers on
Broadway sit up and beg! (*He quotes from Kipling's 'Sestina of the
Tramp-Royal'.*)

Speakin' in general, I 'ave tried 'em all,
The 'appy roads that take you o'er the world.

(*With sodden melancholy.*) Not so apt. Happy roads is bunk.
Weary roads is right. Get you nowhere fast. That's where I've
got – nowhere. Where everyone lands in the end, even if most
of the suckers won't admit it.

EDMUND (*derisively*). Can it! You'll be crying in a minute.

JAMIE (*starts and stares at his brother for a second with bitter hostility –
thickly*). Don't get – too damned fresh. (*Then abruptly.*) But
you're right. To hell with repining! Fat Violet's a good kid.
Glad I stayed with her. Christian act. Cured her blues. Hell of a
good time. You should have stuck with me, Kid. Taken your
mind off your troubles. What's the use coming home to get the

blues over what can't be helped. All over – finished now – not a hope! (*He stops, his head nodding drunkenly, his eyes closing – then suddenly he looks up, his face hard, and quotes jeeringly.*)

If I were hanged on the highest hill,
Mother o'mine, O mother o'mine!
I know whose love would follow me still . . .

EDMUND (*violently*). Shut up!

JAMIE (*in a cruel, sneering tone with hatred in it*). Where's the hophead? Gone to sleep?

EDMUND *jerks as if he'd been struck. There is a tense silence. EDMUND's face looks stricken and sick. Then in a burst of rage he springs from his chair.*

EDMUND. You dirty bastard!

He punches his brother in the face, a blow that glances off the cheekbone. For a second JAMIE *reacts pugnaciously and half rises from his chair to do battle, but suddenly he seems to sober up to a shocked realization of what he has said and he sinks back limply.*

JAMIE (*miserably*). Thanks, Kid. I certainly had that coming. Don't know what made me – booze talking – You know me, Kid.

EDMUND (*his anger ebbing*). I know you'd never say that unless – But God, Jamie, no matter how drunk you are, it's no excuse! (*He pauses – miserably.*) I'm sorry I hit you. You and I never scrap – that bad. (*He sinks back on his chair.*)

JAMIE (*huskily*). It's all right. Glad you did. My dirty tongue. Like to cut it out. (*He hides his face in his hands – dully.*) I suppose it's because I feel so damned sunk. Because this time Mama had me fooled. I really believed she had it licked. She thinks I always believe the worst, but this time I believed the best. (*His voice flutters.*) I suppose I can't forgive her – yet. It meant so much. I'd begun to hope, if she'd beaten the game, I could, too. (*He begins to sob, and the horrible part of his weeping is that it appears sober, not the maudlin tears of drunkenness.*)

EDMUND (*blinking back tears himself*). God, don't I know how you feel! Stop it, Jamie!

JAMIE (*trying to control his sobs*). I've known about Mama so much longer than you. Never forget the first time I got wise. Caught her in the act with a hypo. Christ, I'd never dreamed before that any woman but whores took dope! (*He pauses.*) And then this stuff of you getting consumption. It's got me licked. We've been more than brothers. You're the only pal I've ever had. I love your guts. I'd do anything for you.

EDMUND (*reaches out and pats his arm*). I know that, Jamie.

JAMIE (*his crying over – drops his hands from his face – with a strange bitterness*). Yet I'll bet you've heard Mama and old Gaspard spill so much bunk about my hoping for the worst, you suspect right now I'm thinking to myself that Papa is old and can't last much longer, and if you were to die, Mama and I would get all he's got, and so I'm probably hoping –

EDMUND (*indignantly*). Shut up, you damned fool! What the hell put that in your nut? (*He stares at his brother accusingly.*) Yes, that's what I'd like to know. What put that in your mind?

JAMIE (*confusedly – appearing drunk again*). Don't be a dumbbell! What I said! Always suspected of hoping for the worst. I've got so I can't help – (*Then drunkenly resentful.*) What are you trying to do, accuse me? Don't play the wise guy with me! I've learned more of life than you'll ever know! Just because you've read a lot of highbrow junk, don't think you can fool me! You're only an overgrown kid! Mama's baby and Papa's pet! The family White Hope! You've been getting a swelled head lately. About nothing! About a few poems in a hick town newspaper! Hell, I used to write better stuff for the Lit magazine in college! You better wake up! You're setting no rivers on fire! You let hick town boobs flatter you with bunk about your future –

Abruptly his tone changes to disgusted contrition. EDMUND has looked away from him, trying to ignore this tirade.

Hell, Kid, forget it. That goes for Sweeny. You know I don't mean it. No one is prouder you've started to make good. (*Drunkenly assertive.*) Why shouldn't I be proud? Hell, it's purely selfish. You reflect credit on me. I've had more to do with bringing you up than anyone. I wised you up about women, so you'd never be a fall guy, or make any mistakes you didn't want to make! And who steered you on to reading poetry first? Swinburne, for example? I did! And because I once wanted to write, I planted it in your mind that someday you'd write! Hell, you're more than my brother. I made you! You're my Frankenstein!

He has risen to a note of drunken arrogance. EDMUND is grinning with amusement now.

EDMUND. All right, I'm your Frankenstein. So let's have a
drink. (*He laughs.*) You crazy nut!

JAMIE (*thickly*). I'll have a drink. Not you. Got to take care of
you. (*He reaches out with a foolish grin of doting affection and grabs
his brother's hand.*) Don't be scared of this sanatorium business.
Hell, you can beat that standing on your head. Six months and
you'll be in the pink. Probably haven't got consumption at all.
Doctors lot of fakers. Told me years ago to cut out booze or I'd
soon be dead – and here I am. They're all con men. Anything
to grab your dough. I'll bet this state farm stuff is political graft
game. Doctors get a cut for every patient they send.

EDMUND (*disgustedly amused*). You're the limit! At the Last
Judgement, you'll be around telling everyone it's in the bag.

JAMIE. And I'll be right. Slip a piece of change to the Judge and
be saved, but if you're broke you can go to hell!

He grins at this blasphemy and EDMUND *has to laugh.* JAMIE *goes
on.*

'Therefore put money in thy purse.' That's the only dope.
(*Mockingly.*) The secret of my success! Look, what it's got me!

He lets EDMUND's *hand go to pour a big drink, and gulps it down.
He stares at his brother with bleary affection – takes his hand again
and begins to talk thickly but with a strange, convincing sincerity.*

Listen, Kid, you'll be going away. May not get another chance
to talk. Or might not be drunk enough to tell you truth. So got
to tell you now. Something I ought to have told you long ago –
for your own good.

He pauses – struggling with himself. EDMUND *stares, impressed and
uneasy.* JAMIE *blurts out.*

Not drunken bull, but 'in vino veritas' stuff. You better take it
seriously. Want to warn you – against me. Mama and Papa are
right. I've been rotten bad influence. And worst of it is, I did it
on purpose.

EDMUND (*uneasily*). Shut up! I don't want to hear –

JAMIE. Nix, Kid! You listen! Did it on purpose to make a bum
of you. Or part of me did. A big part. That part that's been
dead so long. That hates life. My putting you wise so you'd
learn from my mistakes. Believed that myself at times, but it's a
fake. Made my mistakes look good. Made getting drunk
romantic. Made whores fascinating vampires instead of poor,

stupid, diseased slobs they really are. Made fun of work as
sucker's game. Never wanted you succeed and make me look
even worse by comparison. Wanted you to fail. Always jealous
of you. Mama's baby, Papa's pet! (*He stares at* EDMUND *with
increasing enmity.*) And it was your being born that started
Mama on dope. I know that's not your fault, but all the same,
God damn you, I can't help hating your guts – !

EDMUND (*almost frightenedly*). Jamie! Cut it out! You're crazy!

JAMIE. But don't get wrong idea, Kid. I love you more than I
hate you. My saying what I'm telling you now proves it. I run
the risk you'll hate me – and you're all I've got left. But I didn't
mean to tell you that last stuff – go that far back. Don't know
what made me. What I wanted to say is, I'd like to see you
become the greatest success in the world. But you'd better be
on your guard. Because I'll do my damnedest to make you fail.
Can't help it. I hate myself. Got to take revenge. On everyone
else. Especially you. Oscar Wilde's 'Reading Gaol' has the dope
twisted. The man was dead, and so he had to kill the thing he
loved. That's what it ought to be. The dead part of me hopes
you won't get well. Maybe he's even glad the game has got
Mama again! He wants company, he doesn't want to be the
only corpse around the house! (*He gives a hard, tortured laugh.*)

EDMUND. Jesus, Jamie! You really have gone crazy!

JAMIE. Think it over and you'll see I'm right. Think it over
when you're away from me in the sanatorium. Make up your
mind you've got to tie a can to me – get me out of your life –
think of me as dead – tell people, 'I had a brother, but he's
dead.' And when you come back, look out for me. I'll be
waiting to welcome you with that 'my old pal' stuff, and give
you the glad hand, and at the first good chance I get stab you
in the back.

EDMUND. Shut up! I'll be God-damned if I'll listen to you any
more – !

JAMIE (*as if he hadn't heard*). Only don't forget me. Remember I
warned you – for your sake. Give me credit. Greater love hath
no man than this, that he saveth his brother from himself. (*Very
drunkenly, his head bobbing.*) That's all. Feel better now. Gone to
confession. Know you absolve me, don't you, Kid? You
understand. You're a damned fine kid. Ought to be. I made
you. So go and get well. Don't die on me. You're all I've got
left. God bless you, K.O.

He falls into a drunken doze, not completely asleep. EDMUND *buries his face in his hands miserably.* TYRONE *comes in quietly through the screen door from the porch, his dressing gown wet with fog, the collar turned up around his throat. His face is stern and disgusted but at the same time pitying.* EDMUND *does not notice his entrance.*

TYRONE (*in a low voice*). Thank God he's asleep.

EDMUND *looks up with a start.*

I thought he'd never stop talking. (*He turns down the collar of his dressing gown.*) We'd better let him stay where he is and sleep it off.

EDMUND *remains silent.* TYRONE *regards him – then goes on.*

I heard the last part of his talk. It's what I've warned you. I hope you'll heed the warning, now it comes from his own mouth.

EDMUND *gives no sign of having heard.* TYRONE *adds pityingly.*

But don't take it too much to heart, lad. He loves to exaggerate the worst of himself when he's drunk. He's devoted to you. It's the one good thing left in him. (*He looks down on* JAMIE *with a bitter sadness.*) A sweet spectacle for me! My first-born, who I hoped would bear my name in honour and dignity, who showed such brilliant promise!

EDMUND (*miserably*). Keep quiet, can't you, Papa?

TYRONE (*pours a drink*). A waste! A wreck, a drunken hulk, done with and finished!

He drinks. JAMIE *has become restless, sensing his father's presence, struggling up from his stupor. Now he gets his eyes open to blink up at* TYRONE. *The latter moves back a step defensively, his face growing hard.*

JAMIE (*suddenly points a finger at him and recites with dramatic emphasis*).

Clarence is come, false, fleeting, perjured Clarence,
That stabbed me in the field by Tewksbury,
Seize on him, Furies, take him into torment.

(*Then resentfully.*) What the hell are you staring at? (*He recites sardonically from Rossetti.*)

Look in my face. My name is Might-Have-Been;
I am also called No More, Too Late, Farewell.

TYRONE. I'm well aware of that, and God knows I don't want to look at it.

EDMUND. Papa! Quit it!

JAMIE (*derisively*). Got a great idea for you, Papa. Put on revival of 'The Bells' this season. Great part in it you can play without make-up. Old Gaspard, the miser!

TYRONE *turns away, trying to control his temper.*

EDMUND. Shut up, Jamie!

JAMIE (*jeeringly*). I claim Edwin Booth never saw the day when he could give as good a performance as a trained seal. Seals are intelligent and honest. They don't put up any bluffs about the Art of Acting. They admit they're just hams earning their daily fish.

TYRONE (*stung, turns on him in a rage*). You loafer!

EDMUND. Papa! Do you want to start a row that will bring Mama down? Jamie, go back to sleep! You've shot off your mouth too much already.

TYRONE *turns away.*

JAMIE (*thickly*). All right, Kid. Not looking for argument. Too damned sleepy.

He closes his eyes, his head nodding. TYRONE *comes to the table and sits down, turning his chair so he won't look at* JAMIE. *At once he becomes sleepy, too.*

TYRONE (*heavily*). I wish to God she'd go to bed so that I could, too. (*Drowsily.*) I'm dog tired. I can't stay up all night like I used to. Getting old – old and finished. (*With a bone-cracking yawn.*) Can't keep my eyes open. I think I'll catch a few winks. Why don't you do the same, Edmund? It'll pass the time until she –

His voice trails off. His eyes close, his chin sags, and he begins to breathe heavily through his mouth. EDMUND *sits tensely. He hears something and jerks nervously forward in his chair, staring through the front parlour into the hall. He jumps up with a hunted, distracted expression. It seems for a second he is going to hide in the back parlour. Then he sits down again and waits, his eyes averted, his hands gripping the arms of his chair. Suddenly all five bulbs of the chandelier in the front parlour are turned on from a wall switch, and a moment later someone starts playing the piano in there – the opening of one of Chopin's simpler waltzes, done with a forgetful, stiff-fingered groping,*

as if an awkward schoolgirl were practising it for the first time.
TYRONE *starts to wide-awakeness and sober dread, and* JAMIE's
head jerks back and his eyes open. For a moment they listen frozenly.
The playing stops as abruptly as it began, and MARY *appears in the*
doorway. She wears a sky-blue dressing gown over her nightdress,
dainty slippers with pompons on her bare feet. Her face is paler than
ever. Her eyes look enormous. They glisten like polished black jewels.
The uncanny thing is that her face now appears so youthful.
Experience seems ironed out of it. It is a marble mask of girlish
innocence, the mouth caught in a shy smile. Her white hair is braided
in two pigtails which hang over her breast. Over one arm, carried
neglectfully, trailing on the floor, as if she had forgotten she held it, is
an old-fashioned white satin wedding gown, trimmed with duchesse
lace. She hesitates in the doorway, glancing round the room, her
forehead puckered puzzedly, like someone who has come to a room to get
something but has become absent-minded on the way and forgotten what
it was. They stare at her. She seems aware of them merely as she is
aware of other objects in the room, the furniture, the windows, familiar
things she accepts automatically as naturally belonging there but which
she is too preoccupied to notice.

JAMIE (*breaks the cracking silence – bitterly, self-defensively sardonic*).
The Mad Scene. Enter Ophelia!

His father and brother both turn on him fiercely. EDMUND *is*
quicker. He slaps JAMIE *across the mouth with the back of his hand.*

TYRONE (*his voice trembling with suppressed fury*). Good boy,
Edmund. The dirty blackguard! His own mother!

JAMIE (*mumbles guiltily, without resentment*). All right, Kid. Had it
coming. But I told you how much I'd hoped – (*He put his hands*
over his face and begins to sob.)

TYRONE. I'll kick you out in the gutter tomorrow, so help me
God. (*But* JAMIE's *sobbing breaks his anger, and he turns and shakes*
his shoulders, pleading.) Jamie, for the love of God, stop it!

Then MARY *speaks, and they freeze into silence again, staring at her.*
She has paid no attention whatever to the incident. It is simply a part
of the familiar atmosphere of the room, a background which does not
touch her preoccupation; and she speaks aloud to herself, not to them.

MARY. I play so badly now. I'm all out of practice. Sister
Theresa will give me a dreadful scolding. She'll tell me it isn't
fair to my father when he spends so much money for extra
lessons. She's quite right, it isn't fair, when he's so good and

generous, and so proud of me. I'll practise every day from now on. But something horrible has happened to my hands. The fingers have gotten so stiff – (*She lifts her hands to examine them with a frightened puzzlement.*) The knuckles are all swollen. They're so ugly. I'll have to go to the Infirmary and show Sister Martha. (*With a sweet smile of affectionate trust.*) She's old and a little cranky, but I love her just the same, and she has things in her medicine chest that'll cure anything. She'll give me something to rub on my hands, and tell me to pray to the Blessed Virgin, and they'll be well again in no time. (*She forgets her hands and comes into the room, the wedding gown trailing on the floor. She glances around vaguely, her forehead puckered again.*) Let me see. What did I come here to find? It's terrible, how absent-minded I've become. I'm always dreaming and forgetting.

TYRONE (*in a stifled voice*). What's that she's carrying, Edmund?

EDMUND (*dully*). Her wedding gown, I suppose.

TYRONE. Christ! (*He gets to his feet and stands directly in her path – in anguish.*) Mary! Isn't it bad enough – ? (*Controlling himself – gently persuasive.*) Here, let me take it, dear. You'll only step on it and tear it and get it dirty dragging it on the floor. Then you'd be sorry afterwards.

She lets him take it, regarding him from somewhere far away within herself, without recognition, without either affection or animosity.

MARY (*with the shy politeness of a well-bred young girl toward an elderly gentleman who relieves her of a bundle.*) Thank you. You are very kind. (*She regards the wedding gown with a puzzled interest.*) It's a wedding gown. It's very lovely, isn't it? (*A shadow crosses her face and she looks vaguely uneasy.*) I remember now. I found it in the attic hidden in a trunk. But I don't know what I wanted it for. I'm going to be a nun – that is, if I can only find – (*She looks around the room, her forehead puckered again.*) What is it I'm looking for? I know it's something I lost. (*She moves back from* TYRONE, *aware of him now only as some obstacle in her path.*)

TYRONE (*in hopeless appeal*). Mary!

But it cannot penetrate her preoccupation. She doesn't seem to hear him. He gives up helplessly, shrinking into himself, even his defensive drunkenness taken from him, leaving him sick and sober. He sinks back on his chair, holding the wedding gown in his arms with an unconscious clumsy, protective gentleness.

JAMIE (*drops his hand from his face, his eyes on the table top. He has suddenly sobered up, too – dully*). It's no good, Papa. (*He recites from Swinburne's 'A Leave-taking' and does it well, simply but with a bitter sadness.*)

Let us rise up and part; she will not know.
Let us go seaward as the great winds go,
Full of blown sand and foam; what help is here?
There is no help, for all these things are so,
And all the world is bitter as a tear.
And how these things are, though ye strove to show,
She would not know.

MARY (*looking around her*). Something I miss terribly. It can't be altogether lost. (*She starts to move around behind* JAMIE'*s chair.*)

JAMIE (*turns to look up into her face – and cannot help appealing pleadingly in his turn*). Mama! (*She does not seem to hear. He looks away hopelessly.*) Hell! What's the use? It's no good. (*He recites from 'A Leave-taking' again with increased bitterness.*)

Let us go hence, my songs; she will not hear.
Let us go hence together without fear;
Keep silence now, for singing-time is over,
And over all old things and all things dear.
She loves not you nor me as all we love her.
Yea, though we sang as angels in the ear,
She would not hear.

MARY (*looking around her*). Something I need terribly. I remember when I had it I was never lonely nor afraid. I can't have lost it for ever. I would die if I thought that. Because then there would be no hope. (*She moves like a sleepwalker, around the back of* JAMIE'*s chair, then forward toward left front, passing behind* EDMUND.

EDMUND (*turns impulsively and grabs her arm. As he pleads he has the quality of a bewilderedly hurt little boy*). Mama! It isn't a summer cold! I've got consumption!

MARY (*for a second he seems to have broken through to her. She trembles and her expression becomes terrified. She calls distractedly, as if giving a command to herself*). No! (*And instantly she is far away again. She murmurs gently but impersonally.*) You must not try to touch me. You must not try to hold me. It isn't right, when I am hoping to be a nun.

He lets his hand drop from her arm. She moves left to the front end of the sofa beneath the windows and sits down, facing front, her hands folded in her lap, in a demure schoolgirlish pose.

JAMIE (*gives* EDMUND *a strange look of mingled pity and jealous gloating*). You damned fool. It's no good. (*He recites from the Swinburne poem.*)

Let us go hence, go hence; she will not see.
Sing all once more together; surely she,
She too, remembering days and words that were,
Will turn a little toward us, sighing; but we,
We are hence, we are gone, as though we had not been there.
Nay, and though all men seeing had pity on me,
She would not see.

TYRONE (*trying to shake off his hopeless stupor*). Oh, we're fools to pay any attention. It's the damned poison. But I've never known her to drown herself in it as deep as this. (*Gruffly.*) Pass me that bottle, Jamie. And stop reciting that damned morbid poetry. I won't have it in my house!

JAMIE *pushes the bottle toward him. He pours a drink without disarranging the wedding gown he holds carefully over his other arm and on his lap, and shoves the bottle back.* JAMIE *pours his and passes the bottle to* EDMUND, *who, in turn, pours one.* TYRONE *lifts his glass and his sons follow suit mechanically, but before they can drink* MARY *speaks and they slowly lower their drinks to the table, forgetting them.*

MARY (*staring dreamily before her. Her face looks extraordinary youthful and innocent. The shyly eager, trusting smile is on her lips as she talks aloud to herself*). I had a talk with Mother Elizabeth. She is so sweet and good. A saint on earth. I love her dearly. It may be sinful of me but I love her better than my own mother. Because she always understands, even before you say a word. Her kind blue eyes look right into your heart. You can't keep any secrets from her. You couldn't deceive her, even if you were mean enough to want to. (*She gives a little rebellious toss of her head – with girlish pique.*) All the same, I don't think she was so understanding this time. I told her I wanted to be a nun. I explained how sure I was of my vocation, that I had prayed to the Blessed Virgin to make me sure, and to find me worthy. I told Mother I had had a true vision when I was praying in the shrine of Our Lady of Lourdes, on the little island in the lake. I said I knew, as surely as I knew I was kneeling there, that the Blessed Virgin had smiled and blessed me with her consent. But Mother Elizabeth told me I must be more sure than that, even that I must prove it wasn't simply my imagination. She said, if I was so sure, then I wouldn't mind putting myself to a test by going home after I graduated and living as other girls lived, going out to parties and dances and enjoying myself; and then if after a year or two I still felt sure, I could come back to see her and we would talk it over again. (*She tosses her head – indignantly.*) I never dreamed Holy Mother would give me such advice! I was really shocked. I said, of course, I would do anything she suggested, but I knew it was simply a waste of time. After I left her, I felt all mixed up, so I went to the shrine and prayed to the Blessed Virgin and found peace again because I knew she heard my prayer and would always love me and see no harm ever came to me so long as I never lost my faith in her. (*She pauses and a look of growing uneasiness comes over her face. She passes a hand over her forehead as if brushing cobwebs from her brain – vaguely.*) That was in the winter of senior year. Then in the spring something happened to me. Yes, I remember. I fell in love with James Tyrone and was so happy for a time.

She stares before her in a sad dream. TYRONE *stirs in his chair.* EDMUND *and* JAMIE *remain motionless.*

Tao House,
20 December, 1940